IGOR PRESNYAKOV'S
FINGERSTYLE GUITAR
ANTHOLOGY

Withdrawn

D0986146

Cover photo: Svjatoslav Presnyakov

Music transcriptions by Pete Billmann, Jeff Jacobson, and Paul Pappas

ISBN 978-1-4950-6896-6

HAL•LEONARD®

7777 W. BLUEMOUND RD. P.O. BOX 13819 MILWAUKEE, WI 53213

For all works contained herein:
Unauthorized copying, arranging, adapting, recording, Internet posting, public performance,
or other distribution of the printed music in this publication is an infringement of copyright.
Infringers are liable under the law.

Visit Hal Leonard Online at
www.halleonard.com

Loveland Public Library
Loveland, CO

Beat It

Words and Music by Michael Jackson

Tune down 1 step:
(low to high) D-G-C-F-A-D

Moderately ♩ = 147

*Hit body of gtr. to create percussive sounds.

**Hit strings near bridge w/ fingers of picking hand,
except where otherwise indicated.

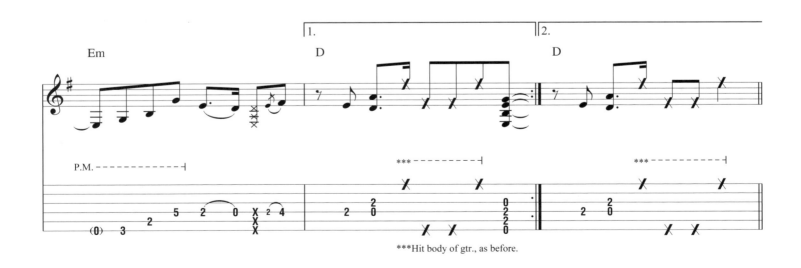

***Hit body of gtr., as before.

Copyright © 1982 Mijac Music
This arrangement Copyright © 2017 Mijac Music
All Rights Administered by Sony/ATV Music Publishing LLC, 424 Church Street, Suite 1200, Nashville, TN 37219
International Copyright Secured   All Rights Reserved

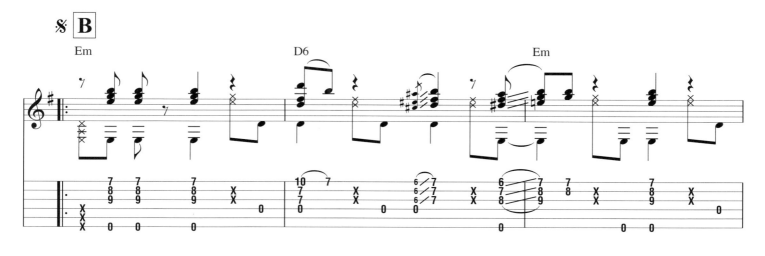

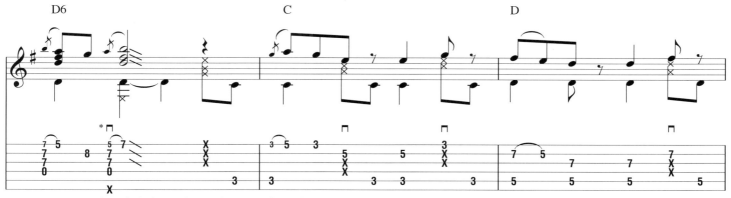

*In a single downstroke, sound upstemmed notes by striking strings
w/ backs of fingernails while slapping thumb against strings to produce
a percussive sound (downstemmed notes), throughout.

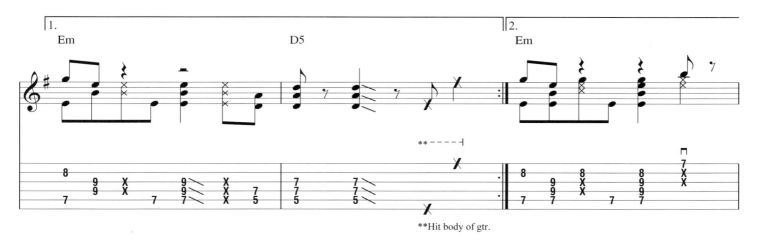

**Hit body of gtr.

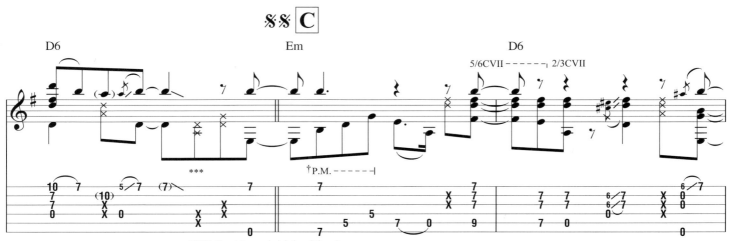

***Strike strings w/ pick-hand thumb.
†Refers to downstemmed notes only.

Em   D6   Em

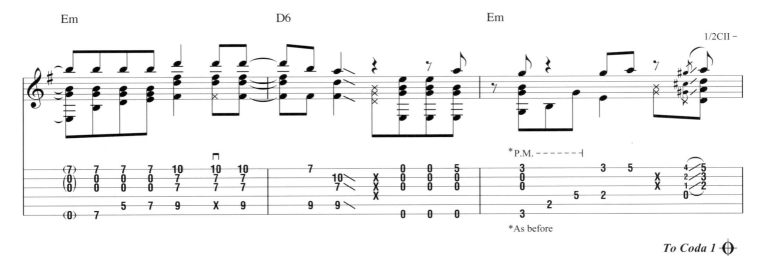

*As before

To Coda 1 ⊕

To Coda 2 ⊕

Dsus2   Em

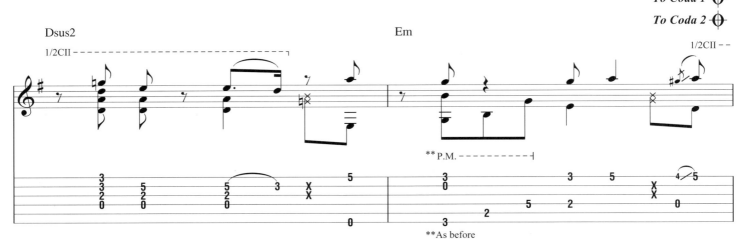

**As before

D.S. al Coda 1
(take repeats)

Dsus2   Em7   E5   D5   D

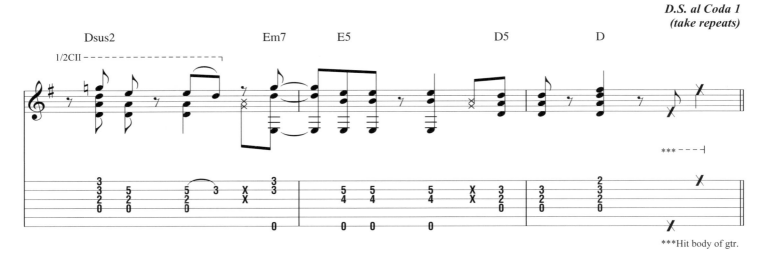

***Hit body of gtr.

⊕ **Coda 1**

Dsus2   Em   D6

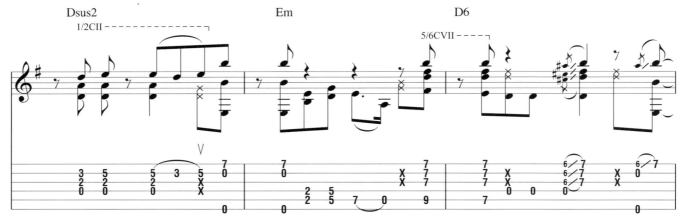

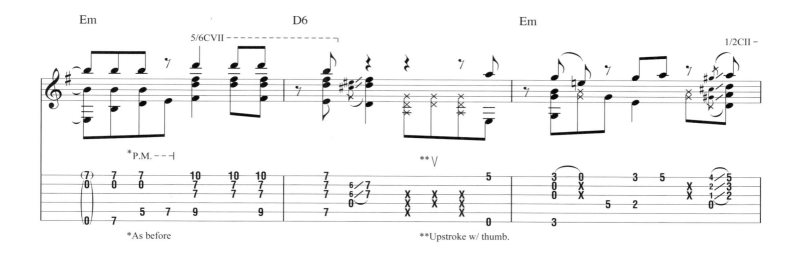

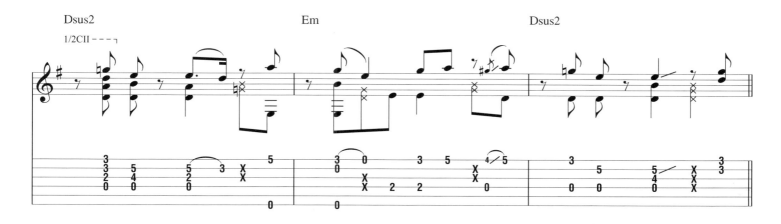

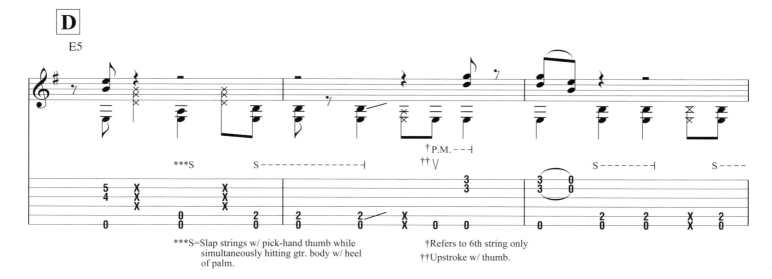

***S=Slap strings w/ pick-hand thumb while
simultaneously hitting gtr. body w/ heel
of palm.

†Refers to 6th string only
††Upstroke w/ thumb.

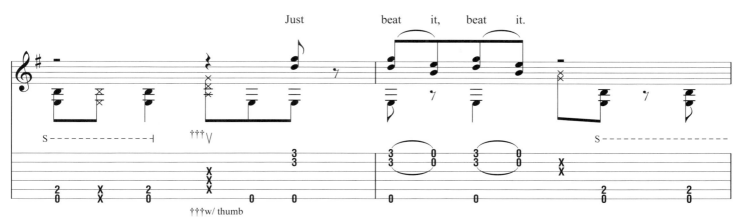

†††w/ thumb

Just   beat   it,   beat   it.

*Hit body of gtr.

E

Em

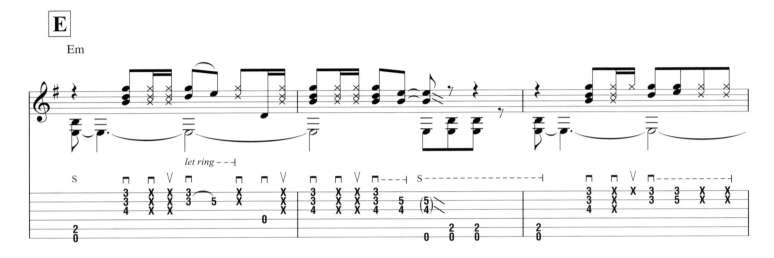

let ring - - ┤

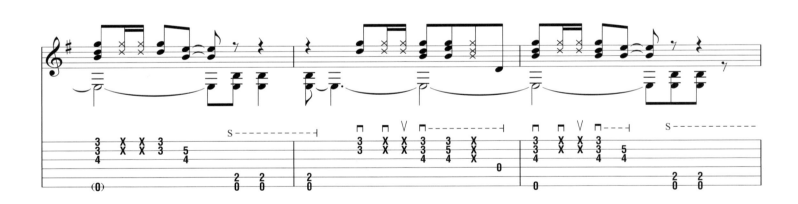

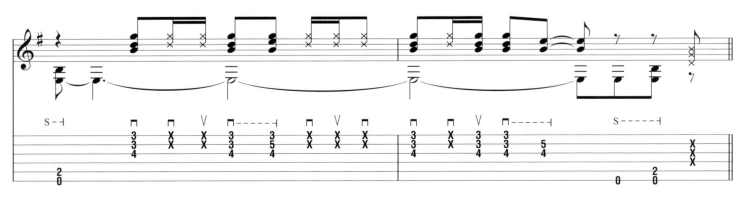

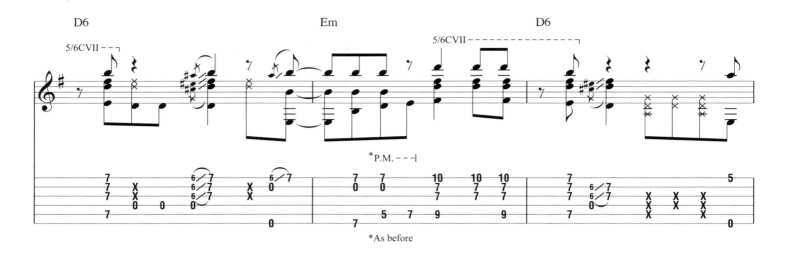

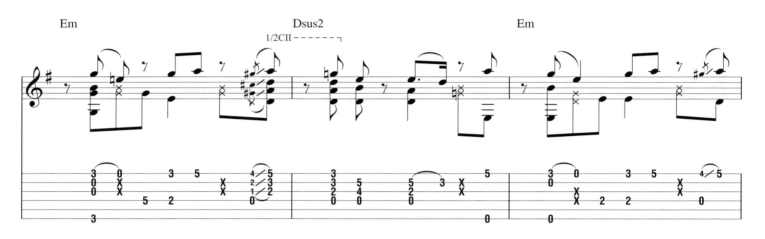

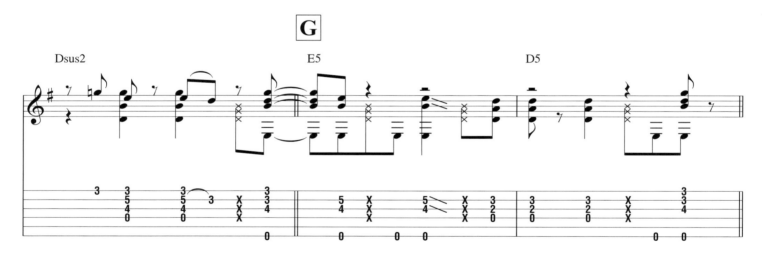

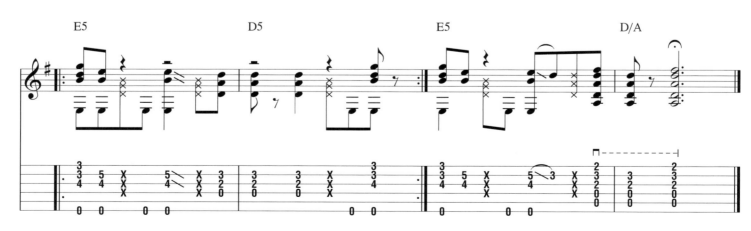

Cancion del Mariachi

Words and Music by Cesar Rosas

Tune down 1 step:
(low to high) D-G-C-F-A-D

Free time

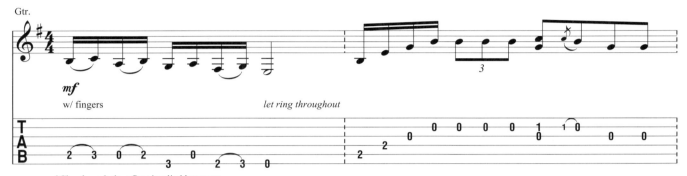

*Chord symbols reflect implied harmony.

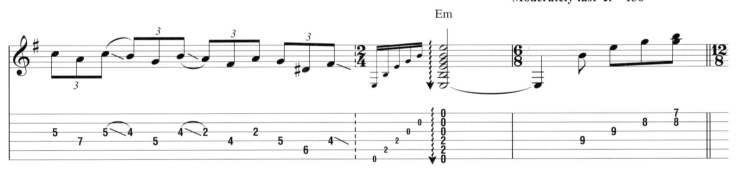

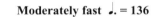

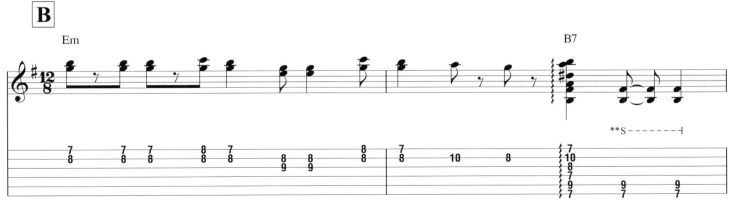

**Slap strings at bridge w/ thumb.

Copyright © 1995 Ceros Music
This arrangement Copyright © 2017 Ceros Music
All Rights Administered by BMG Rights Management (US) LLC
All Rights Reserved   Used by Permission

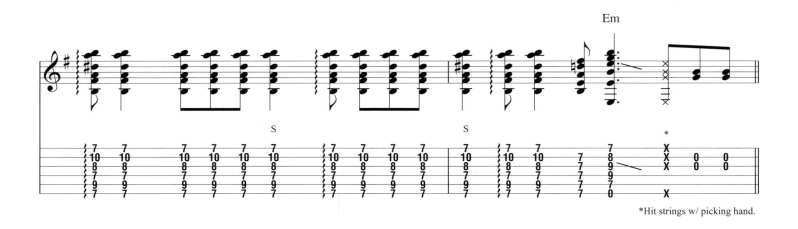

*Hit strings w/ picking hand.

C

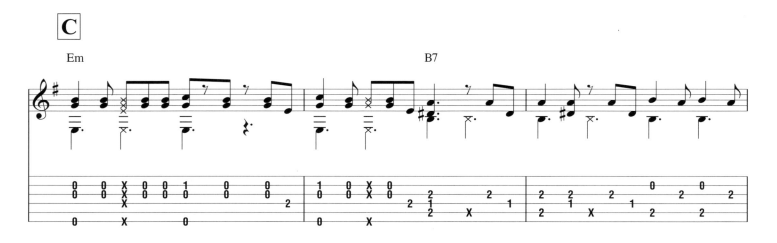

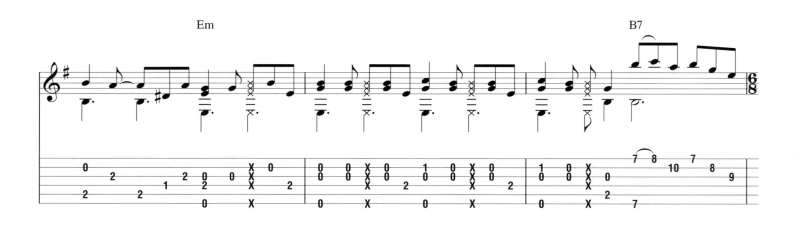

**Refers to upstemmed notes only.

12

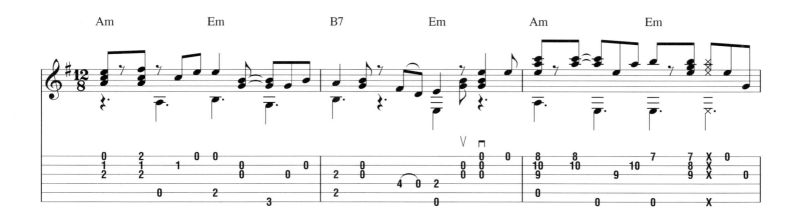

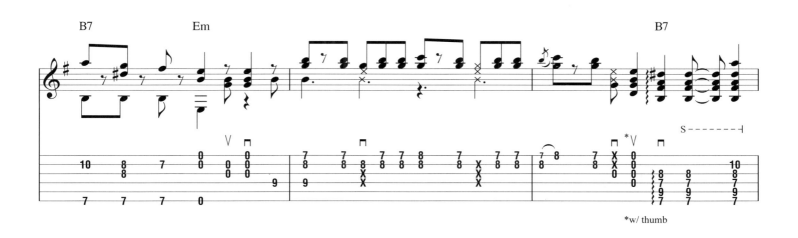

*w/ thumb

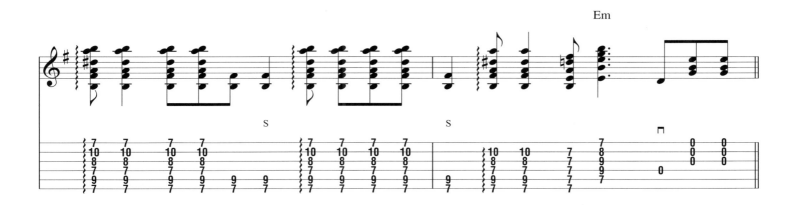

D

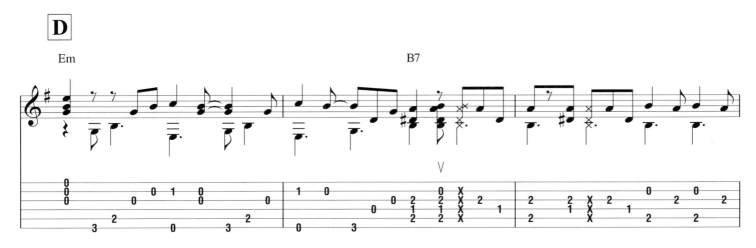

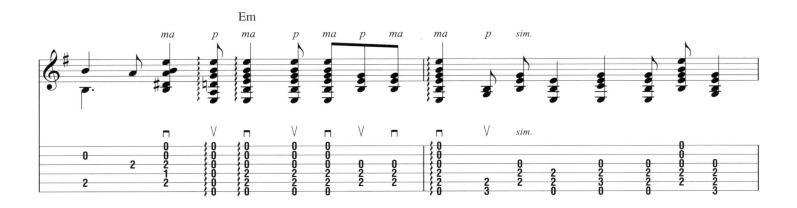

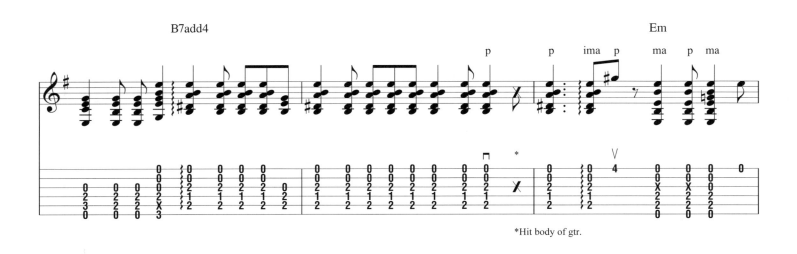

*Hit body of gtr.

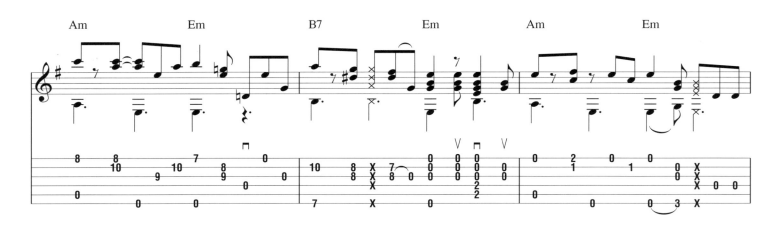

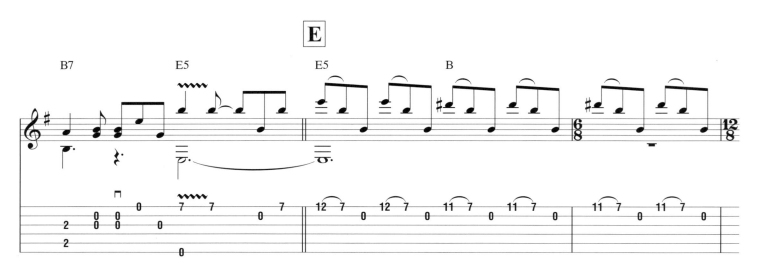

*Hit body of gtr., as before.

*Slap strings w/ palm-side of pick-hand fingers.

**Vary slap location on fretboard to produce occasional random artificial harmonics.

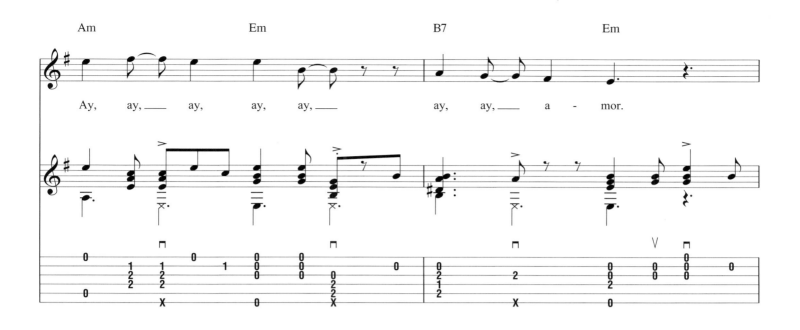

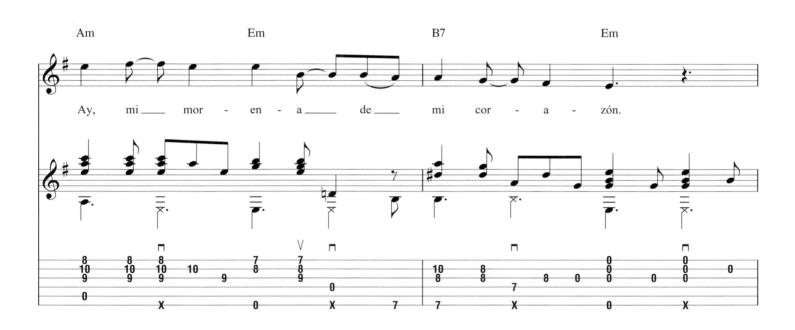

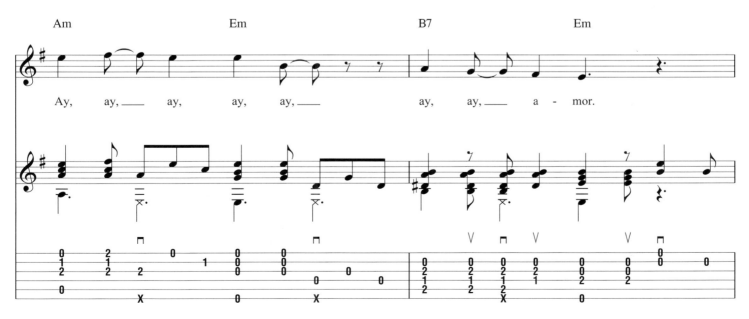

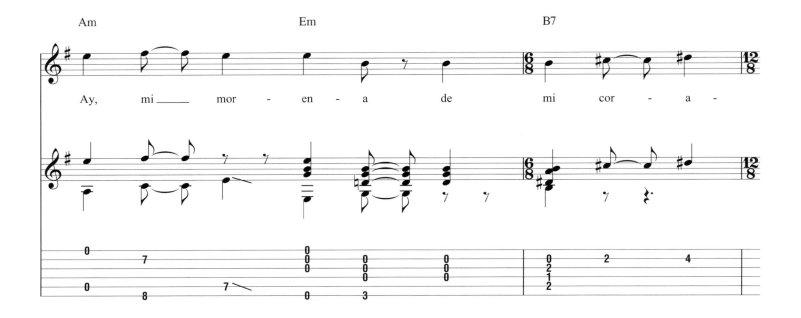

Ay, mi _____ mor - en - a de mi cor - a -

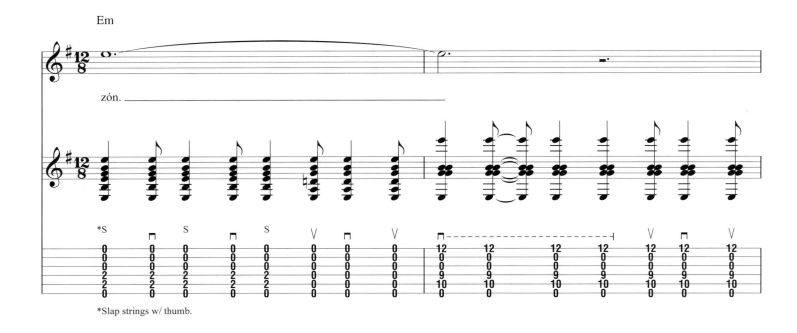

zón. _____

*Slap strings w/ thumb.

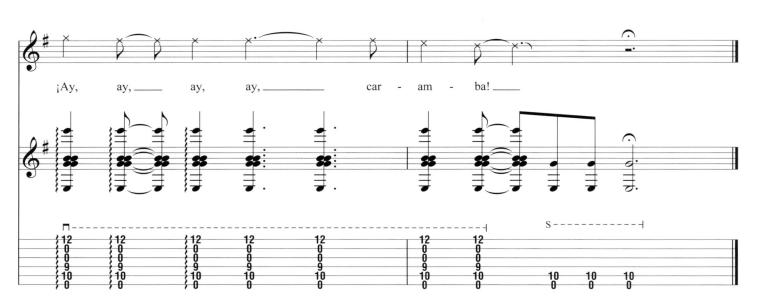

¡Ay, ay, _____ ay, ay, _____ car - am - ba! _____

Don't Cry

Words and Music by Izzy Stradlin' and W. Axl Rose

Tune down 1 step:
(low to high) D-G-C-F-A-D

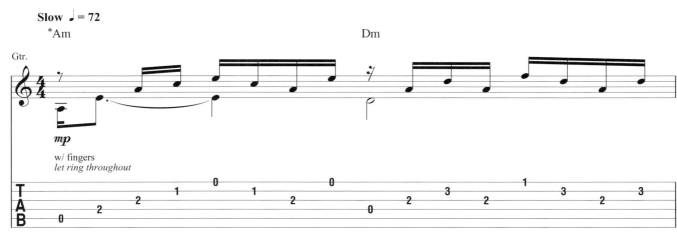

*Chord symbols reflect basic harmony.

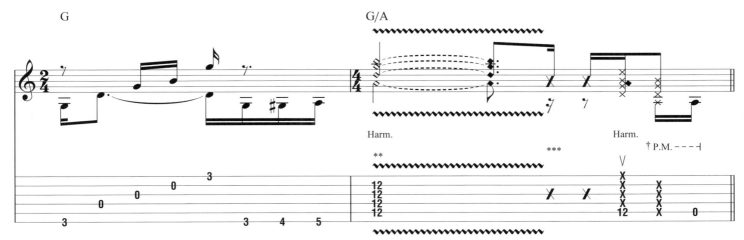

**Shake neck at headstock w/ fretting hand
to create slight vibrato.

***Hit body of gtr.

†Hit strings simultaneously
w/ thumb & back of fingernails,
producing a percussive sound,
throughout.

Copyright © 1991 Guns N' Roses Music (ASCAP) and Black Frog Music (ASCAP)
This arrangement Copyright © 2017 Guns N' Roses Music (ASCAP) and Black Frog Music (ASCAP)
All Rights for Black Frog Music in the U.S. and Canada Controlled and Administered by Universal - PolyGram International Publishing, Inc.
International Copyright Secured   All Rights Reserved

B

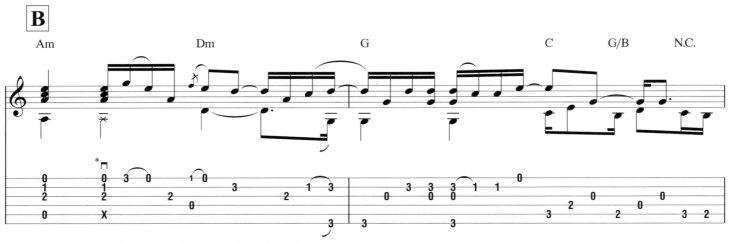

*In a single downstroke, sound upstemmed notes by striking strings
 w/ backs of fingernails while slapping thumb against strings to produce
 a percussive sound (downstemmed notes), throughout.

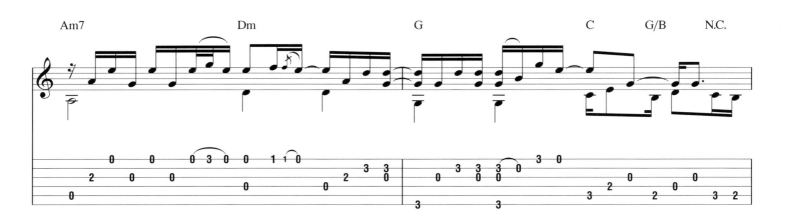

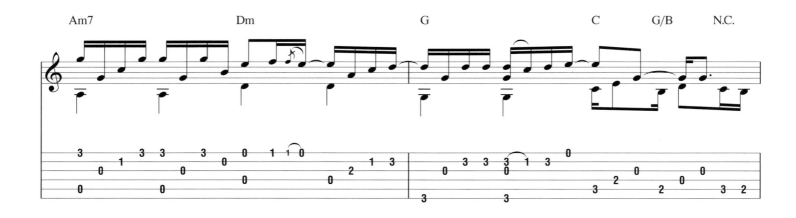

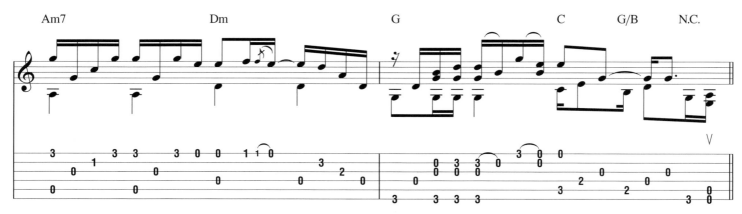

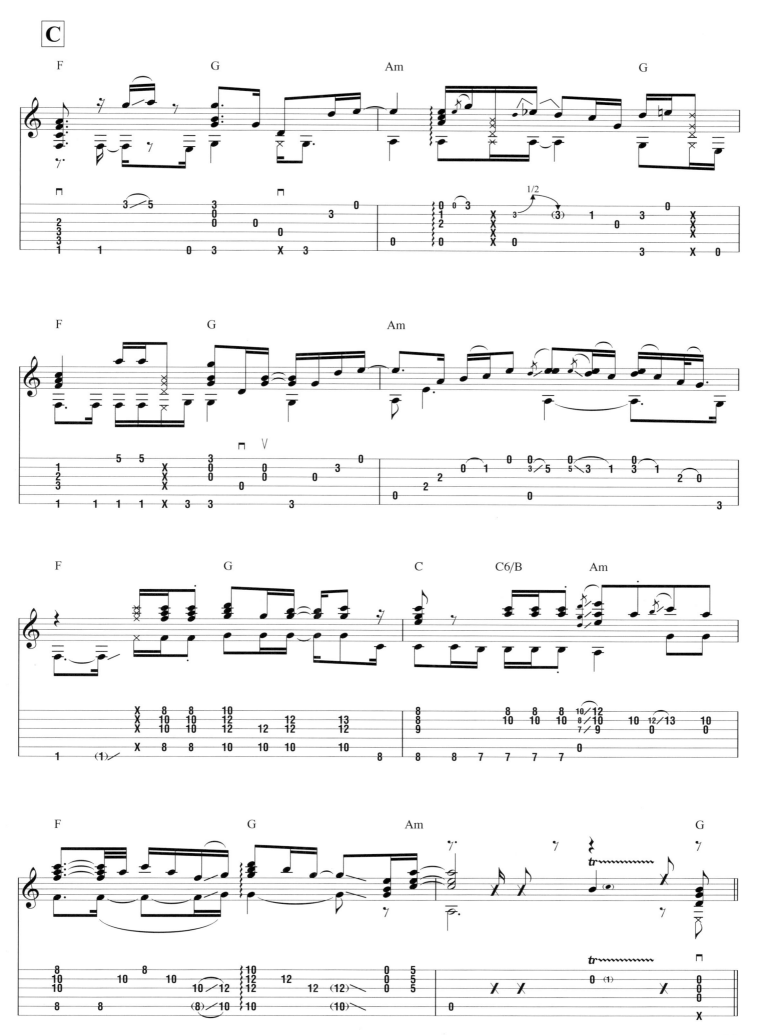

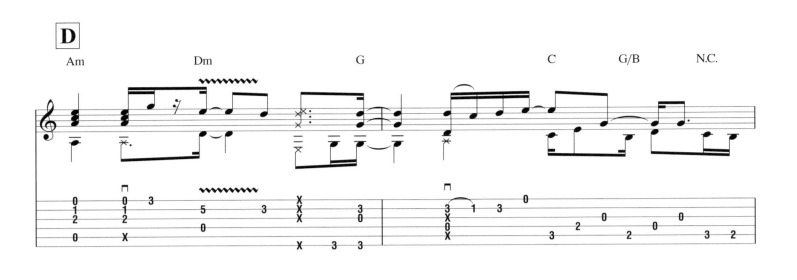

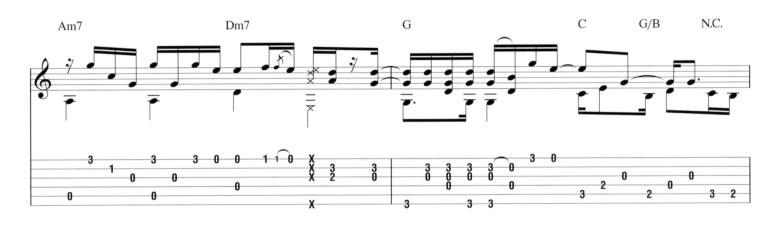

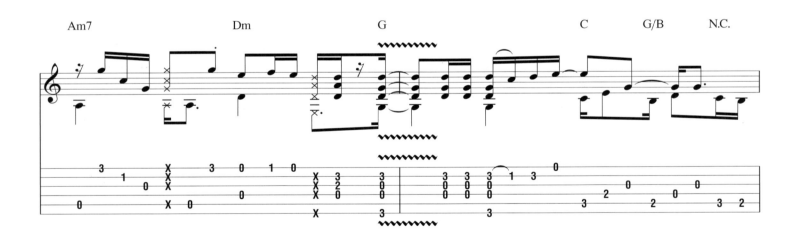

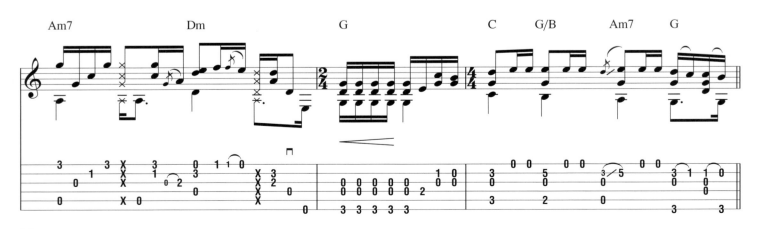

E

*Lightly tap soundboard w/ fingers (golpe).

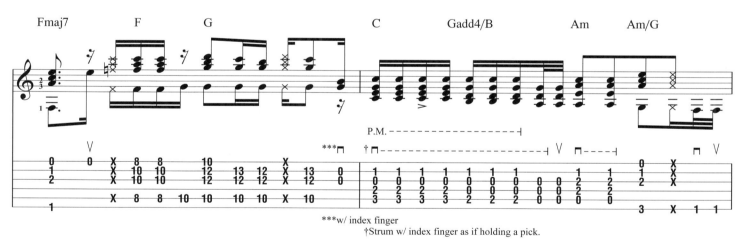

**P.M.

**Refers to
downstemmed
note only.

***w/ index finger
†Strum w/ index finger as if holding a pick.

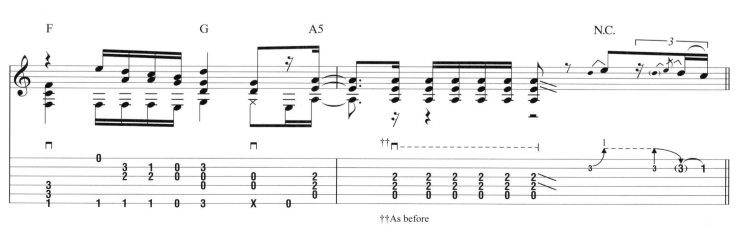

††As before

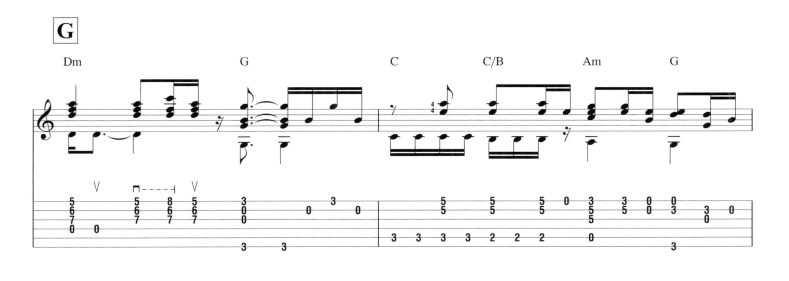

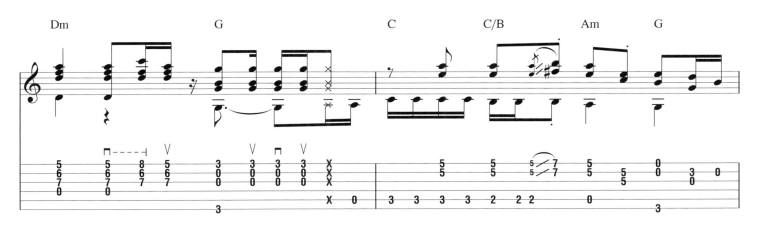

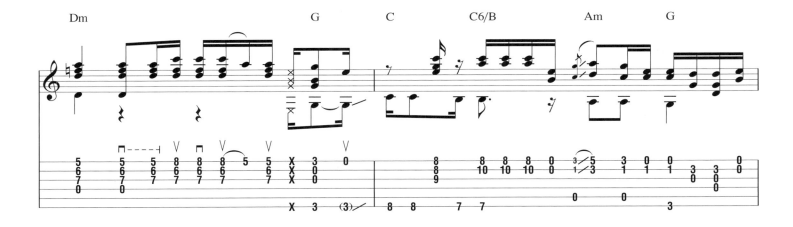

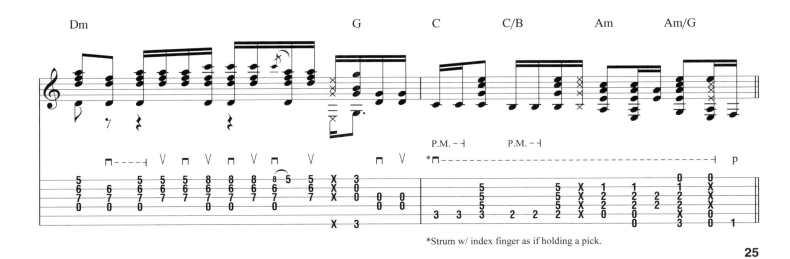

*Strum w/ index finger as if holding a pick.

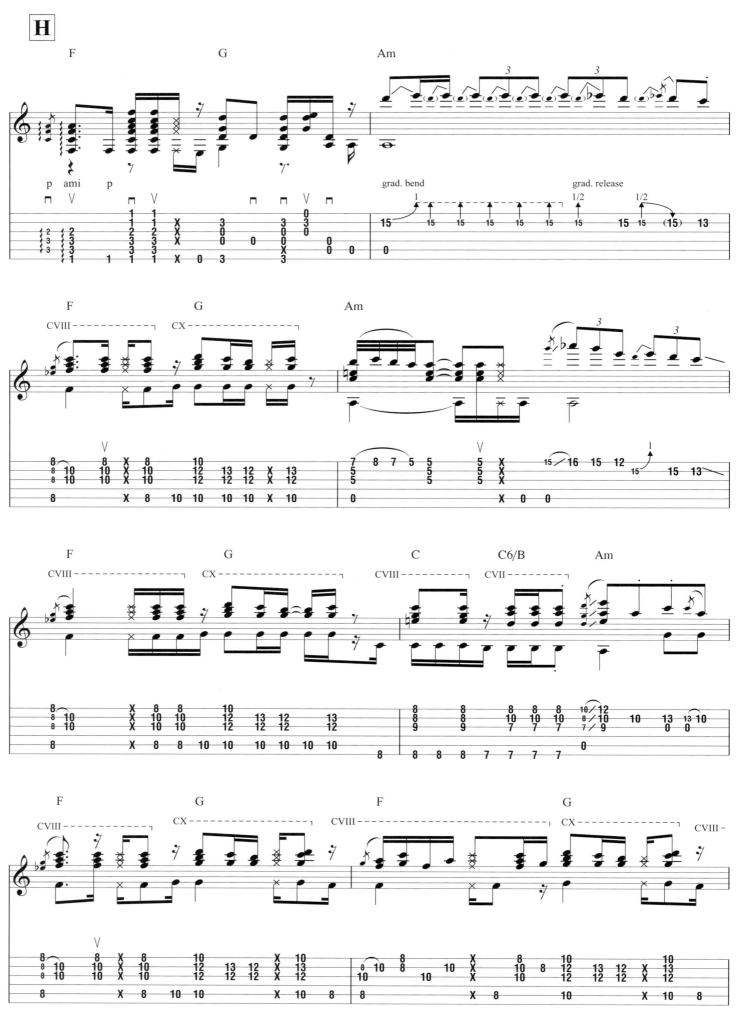

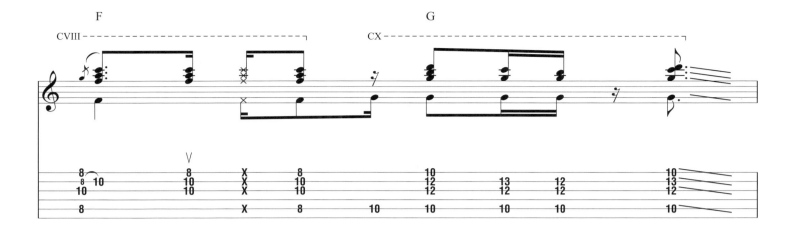

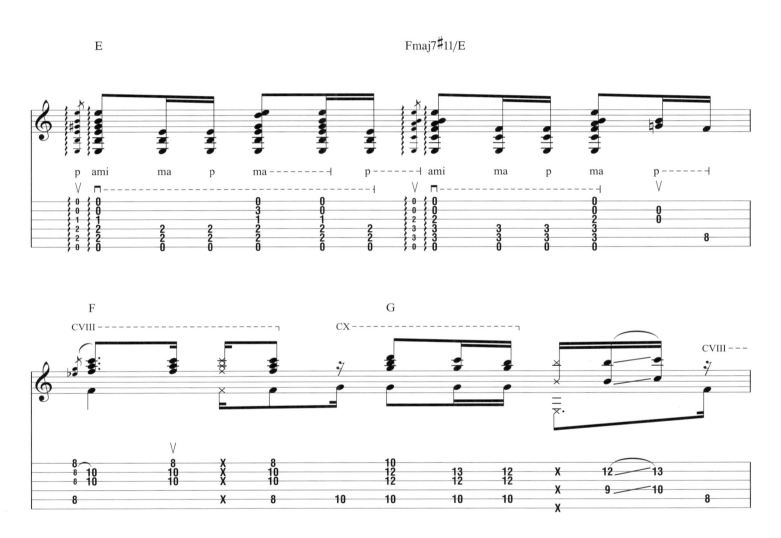

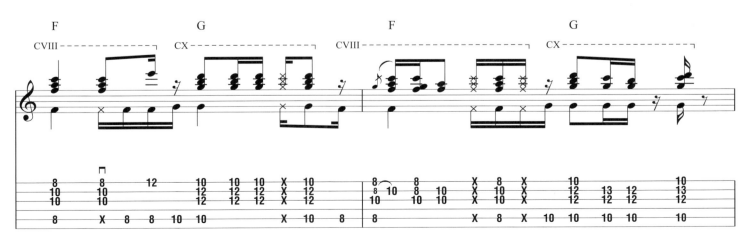

Free time

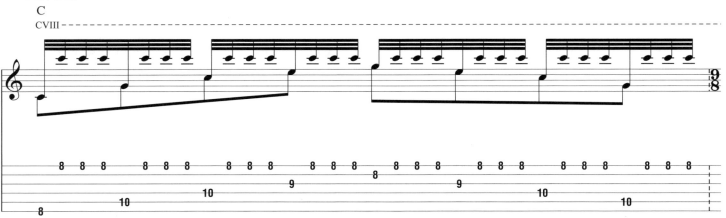

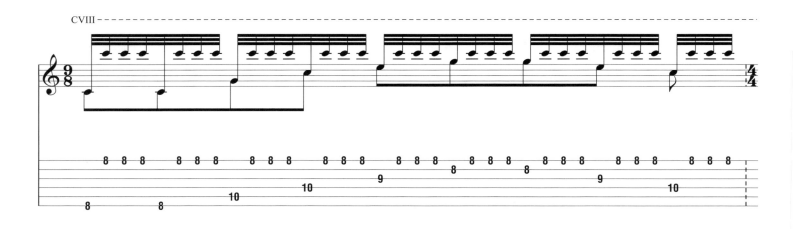

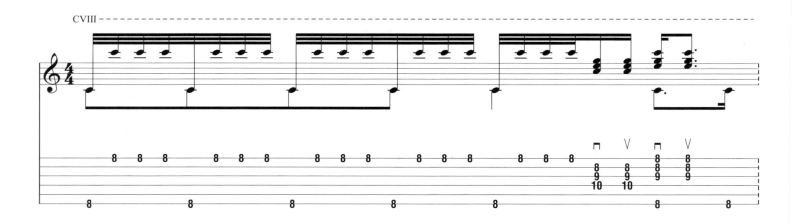

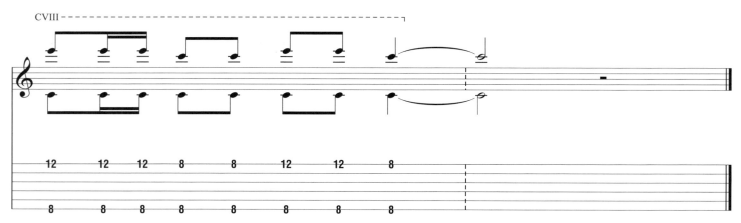

Dust in the Wind

Words and Music by Kerry Livgren

Tune down 1 step:
(low to high) D-G-C-F-A-D

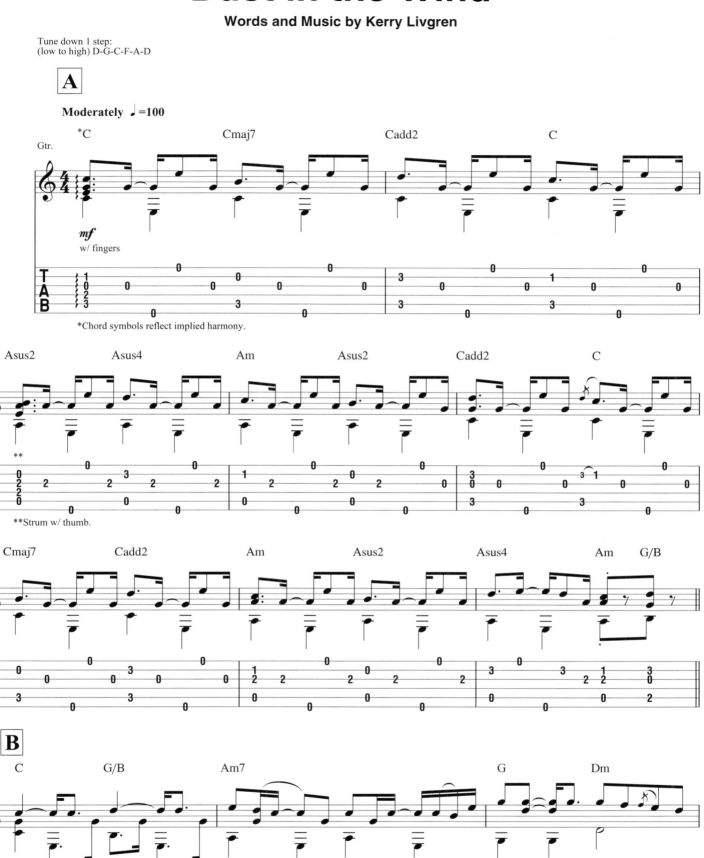

Copyright © 1977, 1978 EMI Blackwood Music Inc. and Don Kirshner Music
Copyright Renewed
This arrangement Copyright © 2017 EMI Blackwood Music Inc. and Don Kirshner Music
All Rights Administered by Sony/ATV Music Publishing LLC, 424 Church Street, Suite 1200, Nashville, TN 37219
International Copyright Secured All Rights Reserved

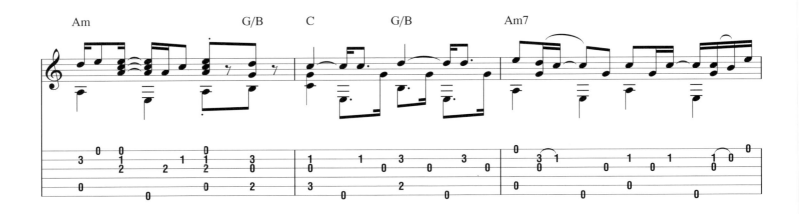

C

*Lightly hit strings.

D

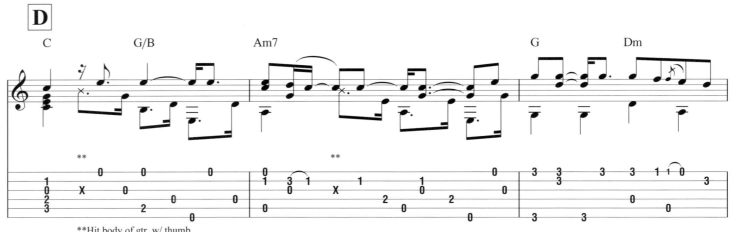

**Hit body of gtr. w/ thumb.

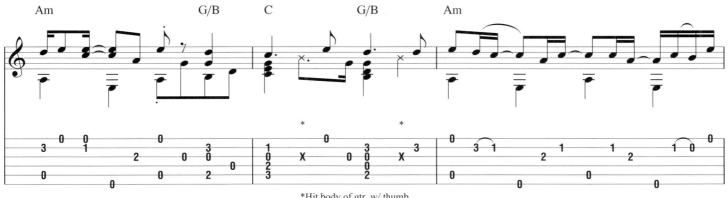

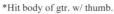
*Hit body of gtr. w/ thumb.

E

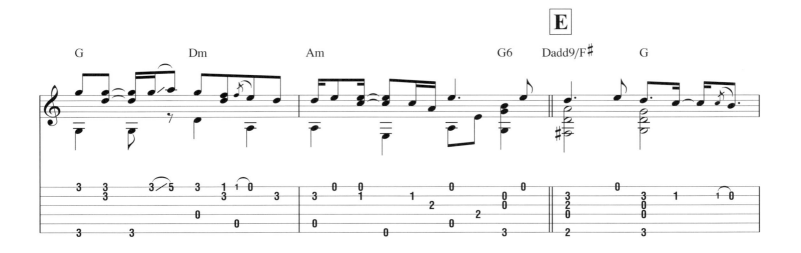

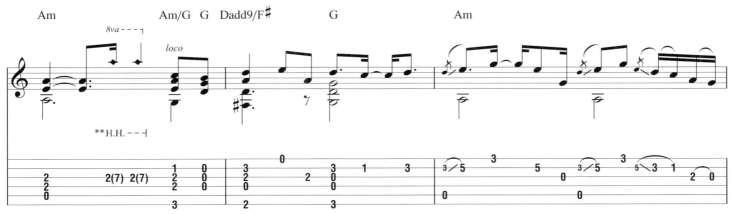

**Harp harmonics achieved by lightly touching string w/ picking-hand
index finger at fret indicated in parentheses and plucking with thumb.

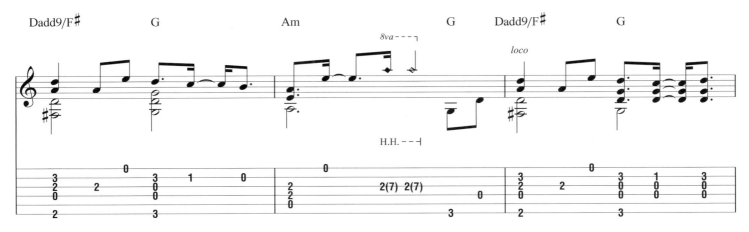

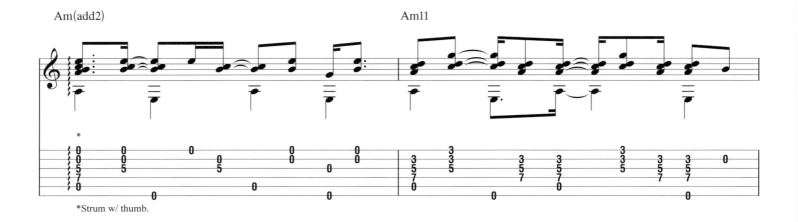

*Strum w/ thumb.

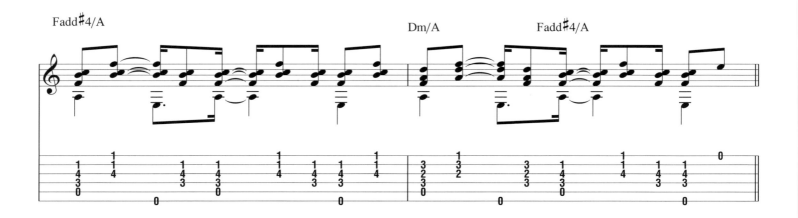

**As before

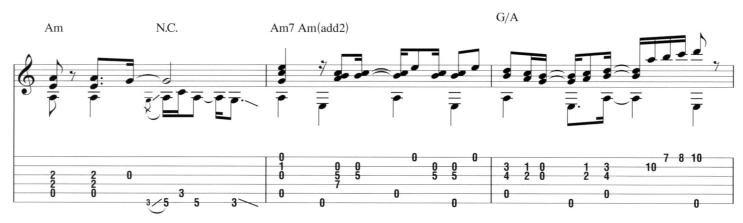

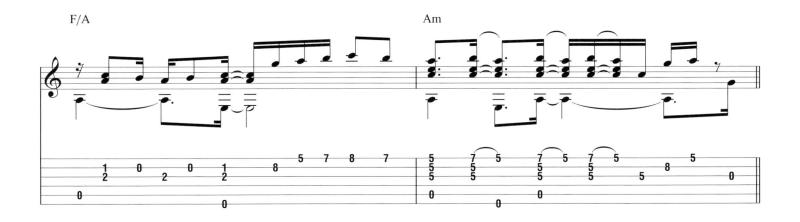

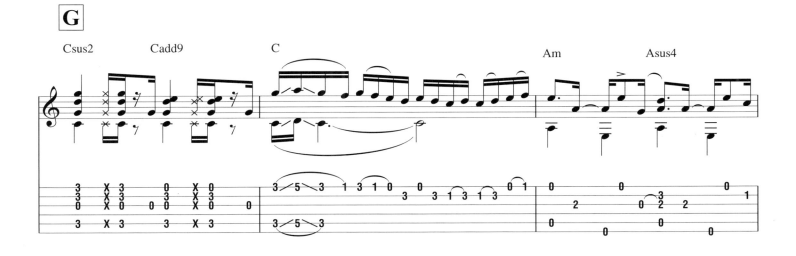

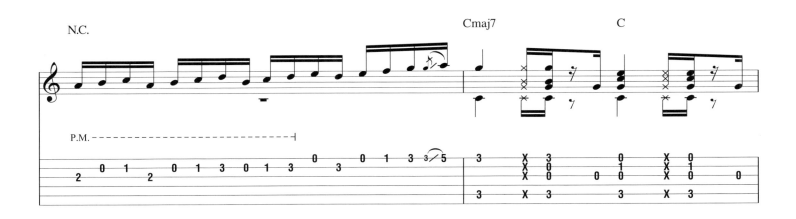

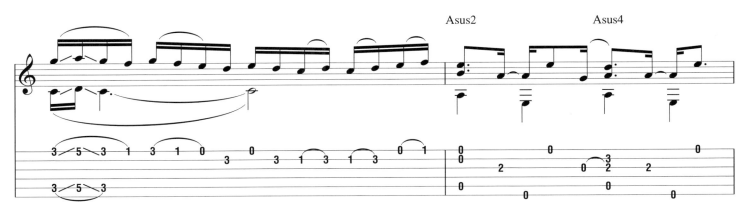

H

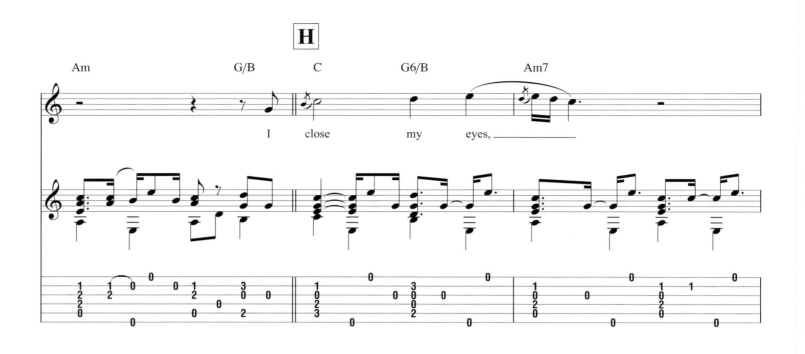

I close my eyes,

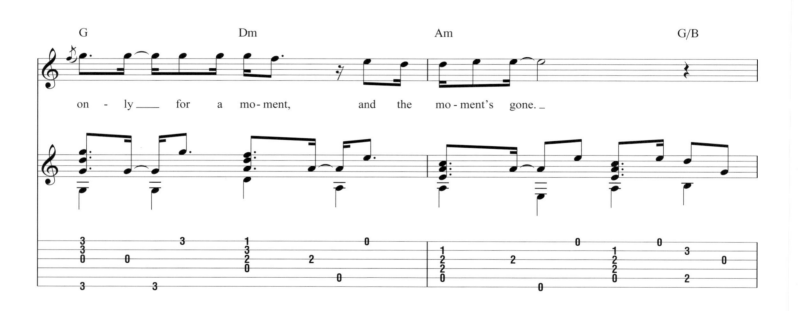

on - ly ___ for a mo - ment, and the mo - ment's gone. _

All my dreams ___

34

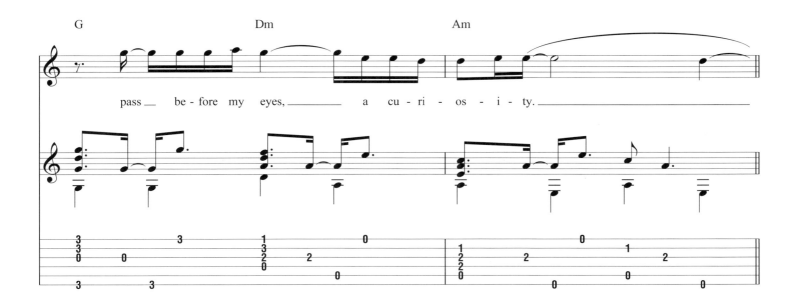

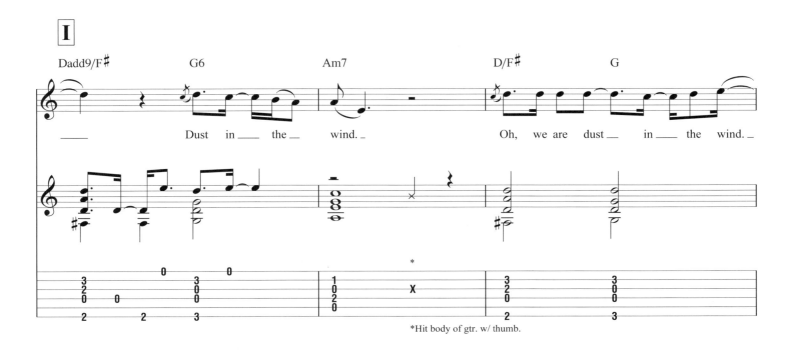

*Hit body of gtr. w/ thumb.

**As before.

Oh,   we   are   dust _____ in ____ the   wind. _

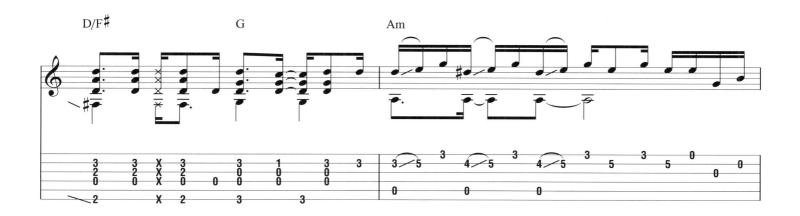

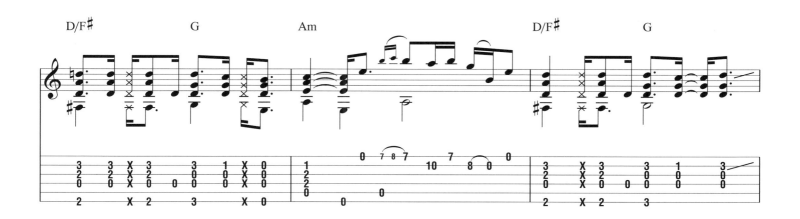

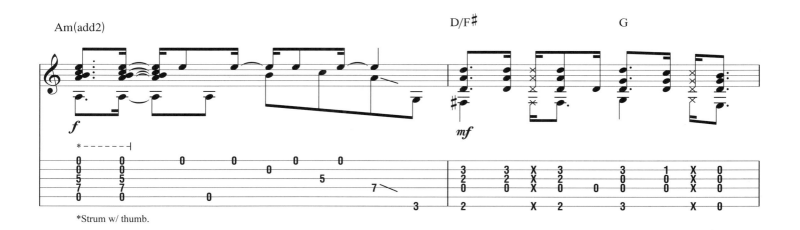

*Strum w/ thumb.

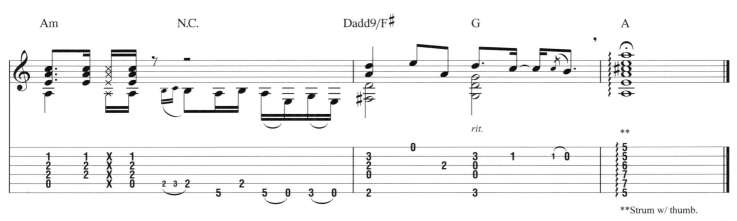

**Strum w/ thumb.

Every Breath You Take

Music and Lyrics by Sting

Tune down 1/2 step, capo II:
(low to high) Eb-Ab-Db-Gb-Bb-Eb

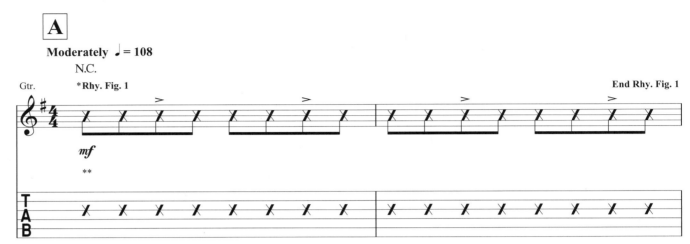

*Rhy. Fig. 1 is created as a loop using a looper pedal.

**Slap strings over soundhole w/ pick-hand
  fingers to produce a percussive sound.

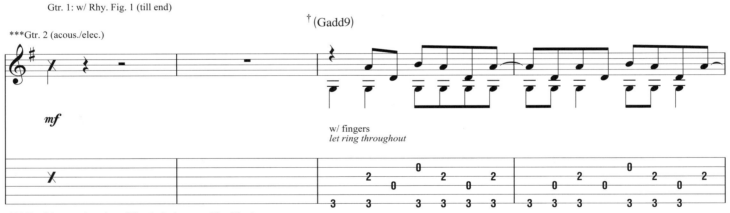

***Gtr. 2 is a continuation of Gtr. 1 playing over Rhy. Fig. 1

†Symbols in parentheses represent chord symbols respective to capoed gtr.
  Capoed fret is "0" in tab. Chord symbols reflect implied harmony.

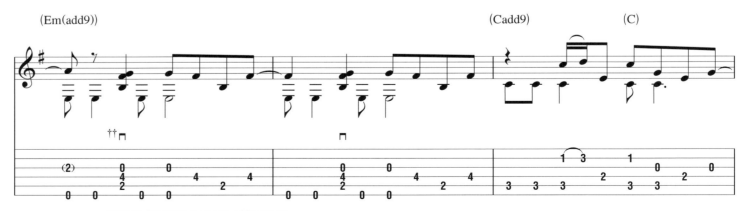

††Single downstroke w/ backs of fingernails,
  throughout except where indicated.

Copyright © 1983 G.M. Sumner
This arrangement Copyright © 2017 G.M. Sumner
All Rights Administered by Sony/ATV Music Publishing LLC, 424 Church Street, Suite 1200, Nashville, TN 37219
International Copyright Secured   All Rights Reserved

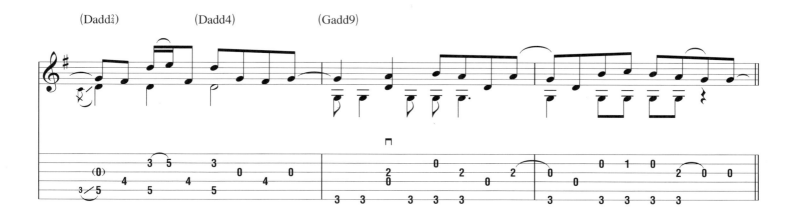

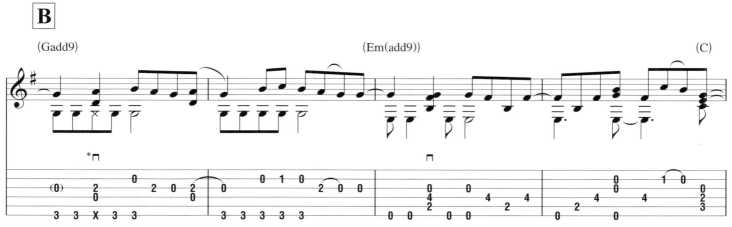

*In a single downstroke, sound upstemmed notes by striking strings w/ backs of fingernails
while slapping thumb against strings to produce a percussive sound (downstemmed notes), throughout.

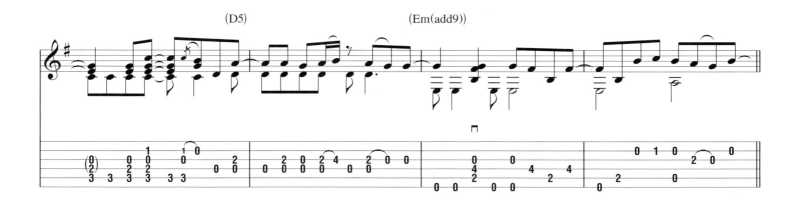

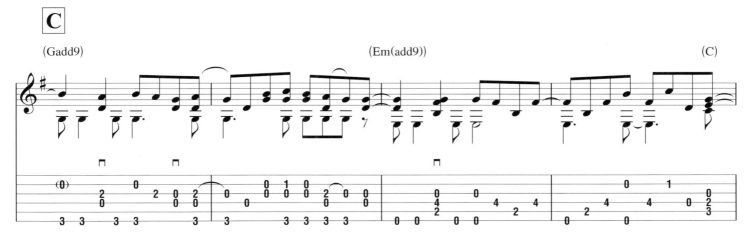

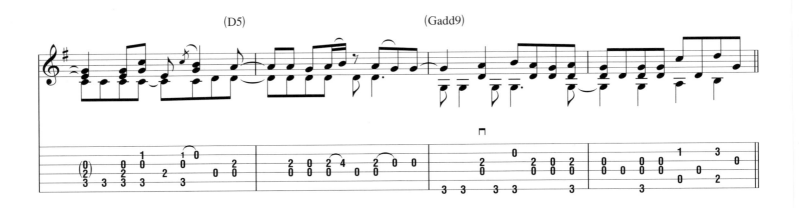

D

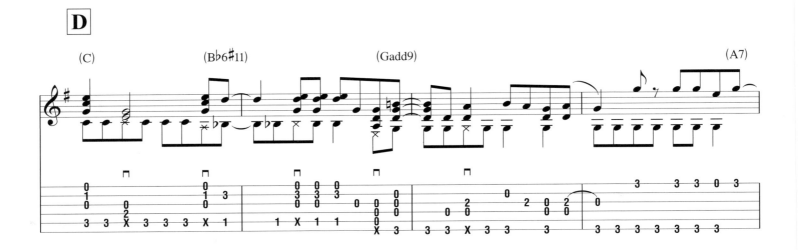

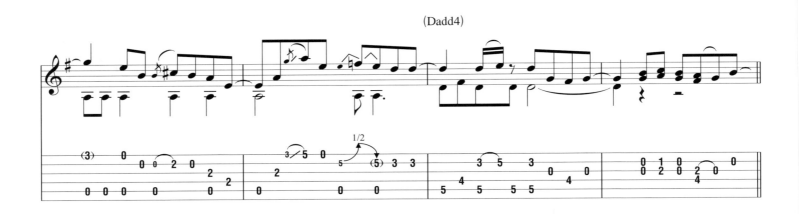

E

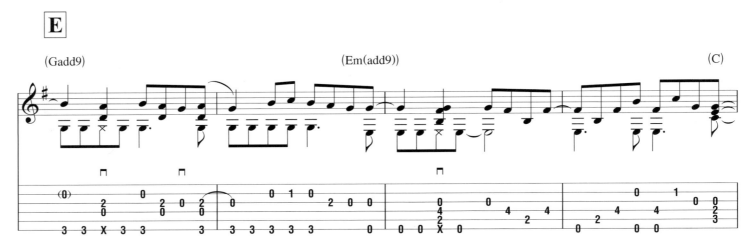

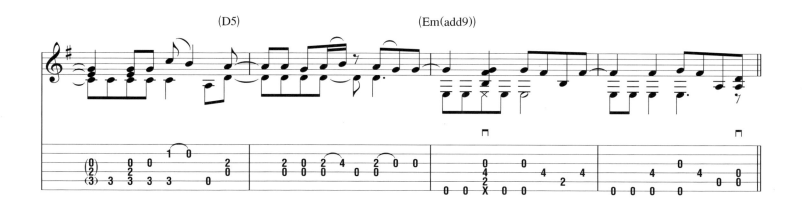

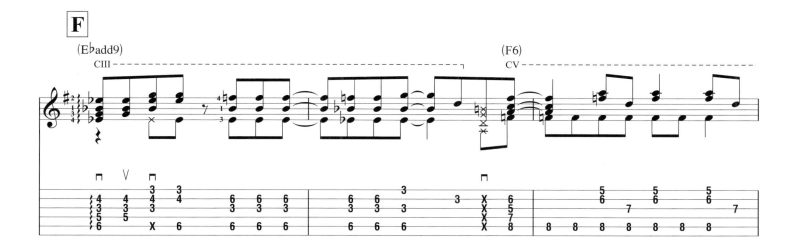

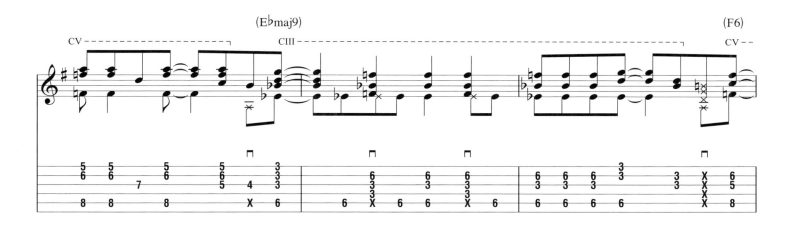

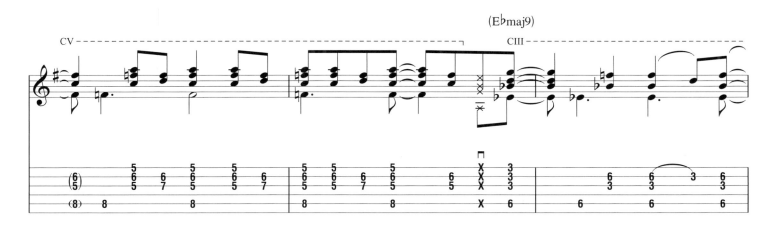

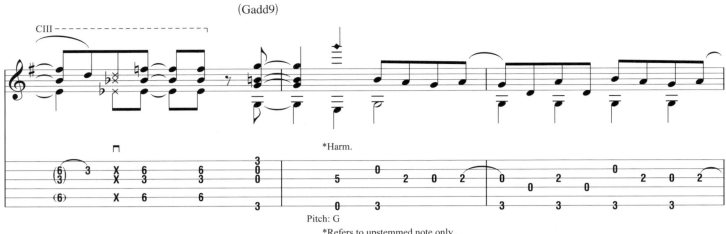

(Gadd9)

*Harm.

Pitch: G

*Refers to upstemmed note only.

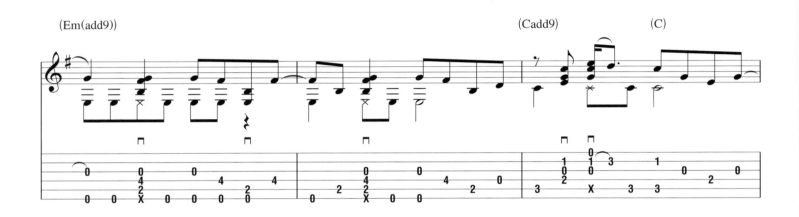

(Em(add9))   (Cadd9)   (C)

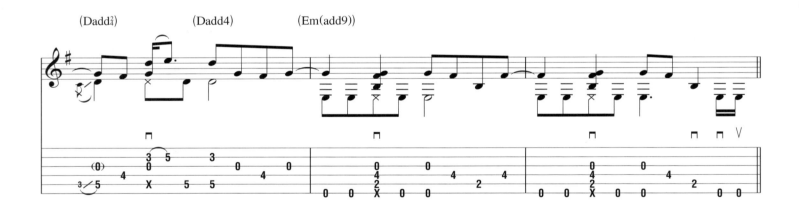

(Dadd⅔)   (Dadd4)   (Em(add9))

G

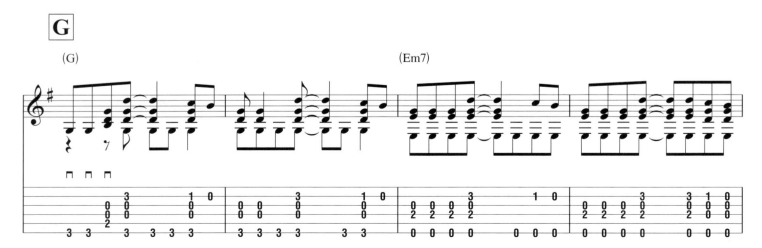

(G)   (Em7)

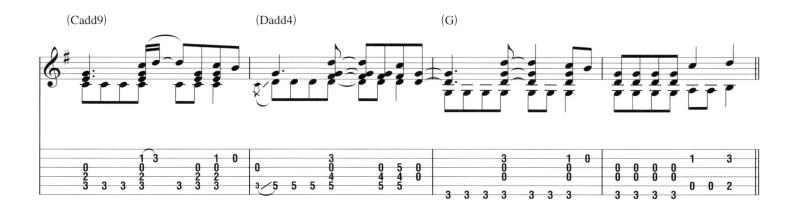

H

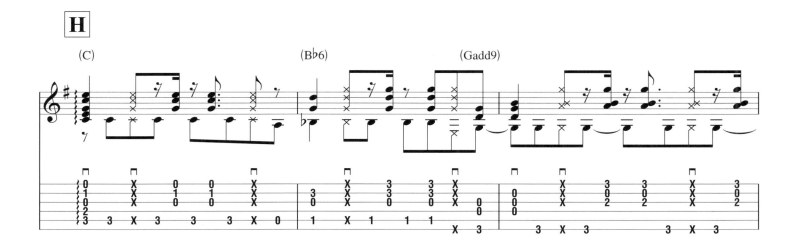

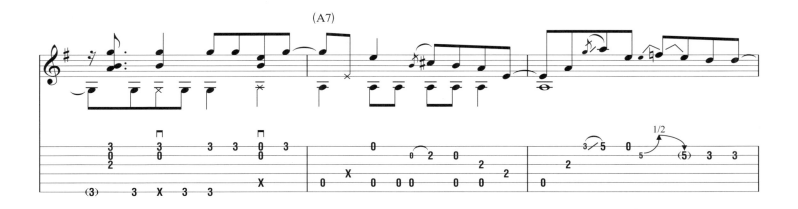

I

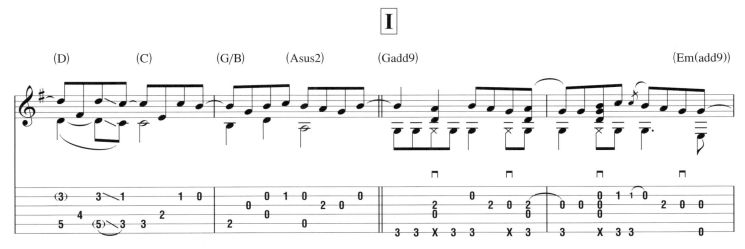

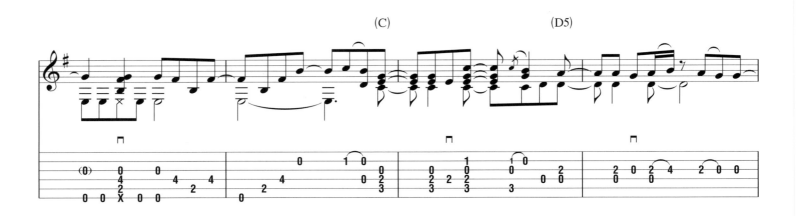

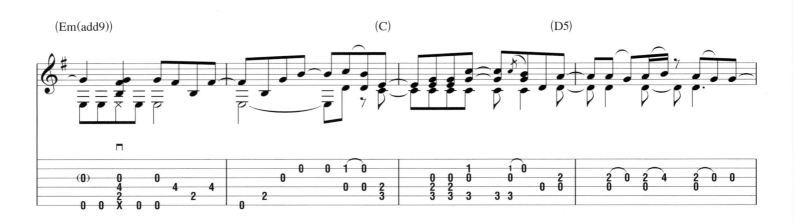

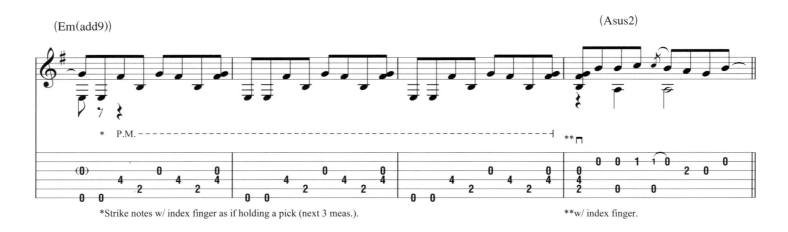

*Strike notes w/ index finger as if holding a pick (next 3 meas.).   **w/ index finger.

J

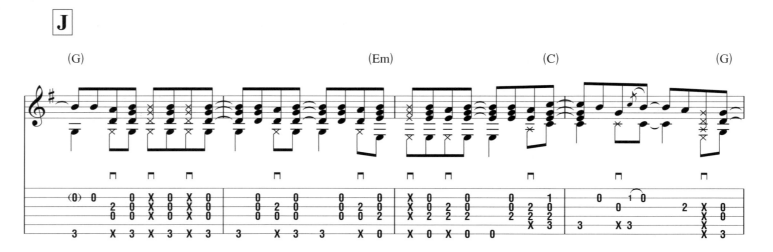

44

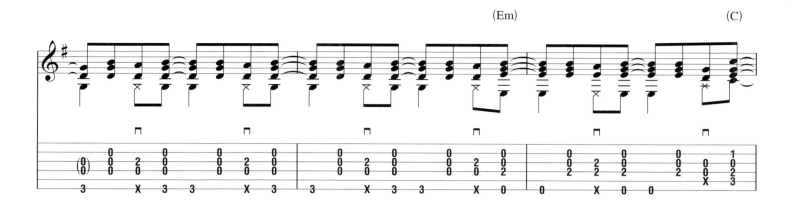

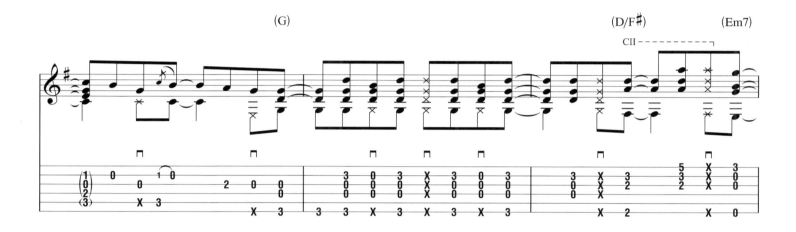

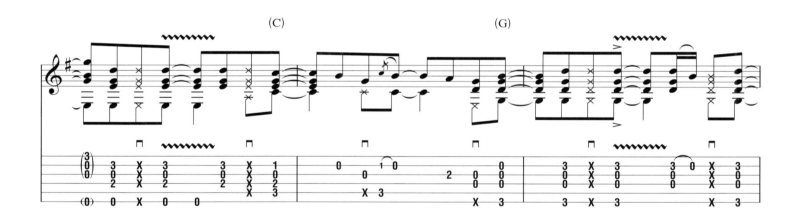

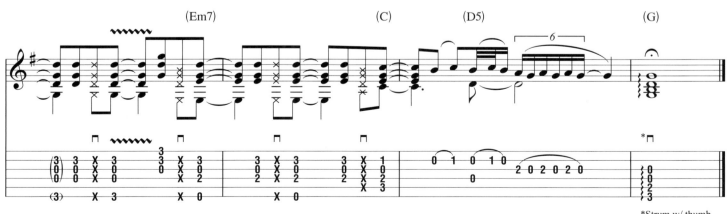

*Strum w/ thumb.

He's a Pirate

from PIRATES OF THE CARIBBEAN: THE CURSE OF THE BLACK PEARL

Music by Klaus Badelt

Drop D tuning, down 1 step:
(low to high) C-G-C-F-A-D

Moderately fast ♩. = 135

*Chord symbols reflect implied harmony.

**While continuing to fingerpick open D string, hit body of gtr. w/ fret-hand fingers.

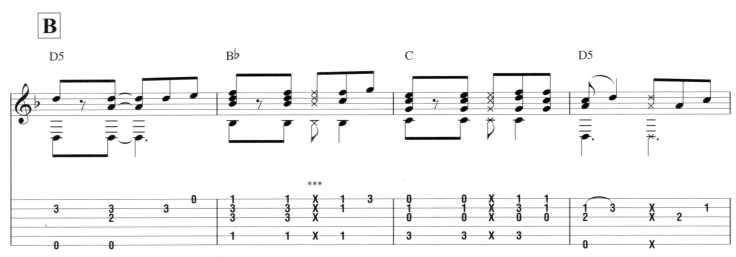

***Simultaneously hit strings w/ thumb & backs of fingernails to produce a percussive sound, throughout.

© 2003 Walt Disney Music Company
This arrangement © 2017 Walt Disney Music Company
All Rights Reserved. Used by Permission.

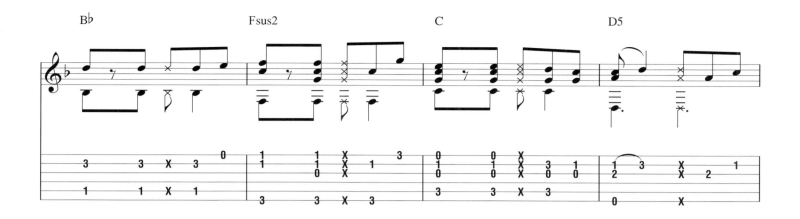

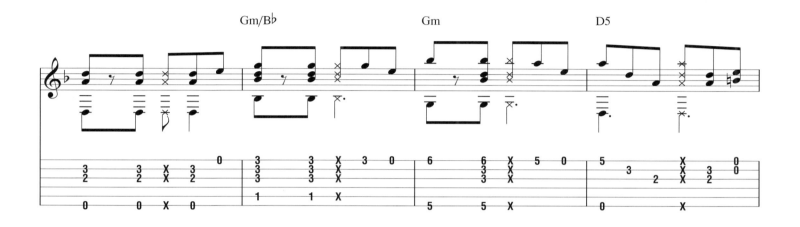

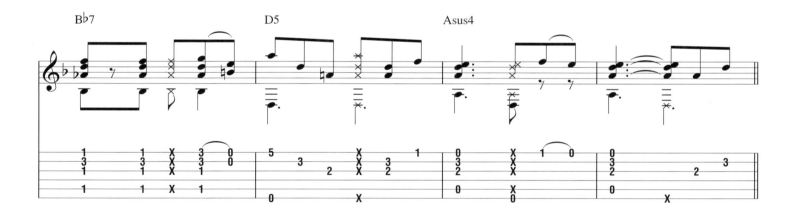

C

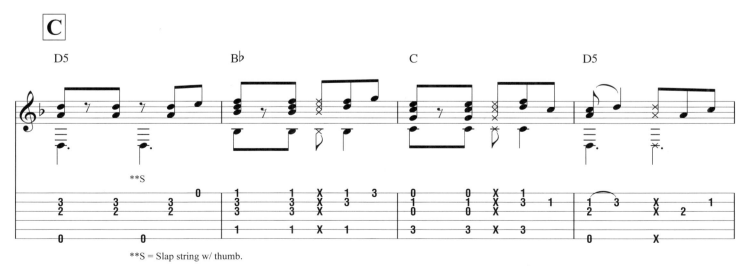

**S = Slap string w/ thumb.

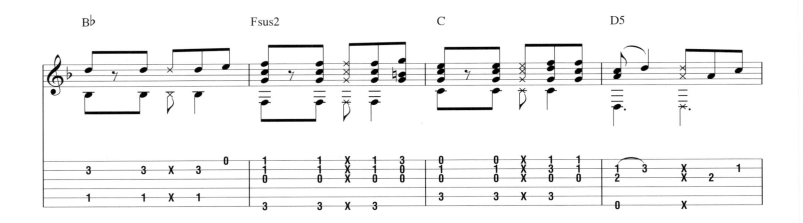

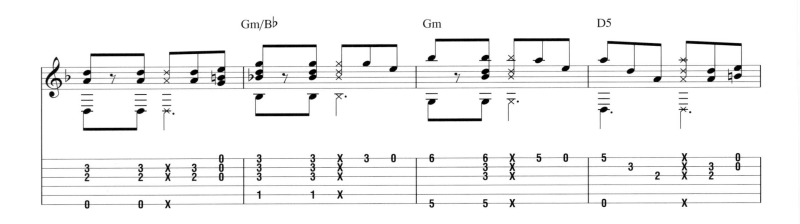

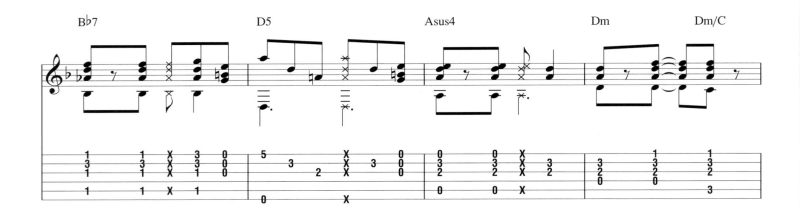

D

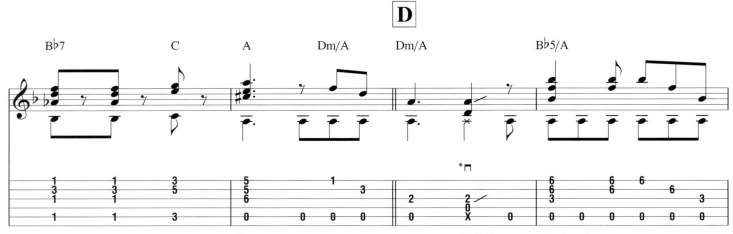

*Refers to upstemmed notes only.

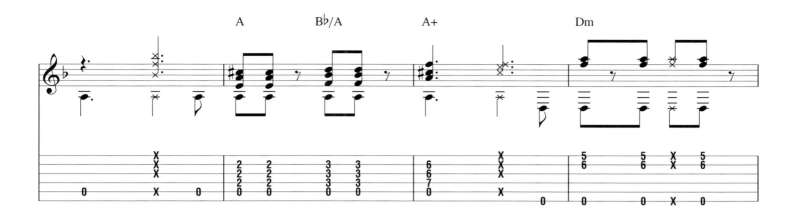

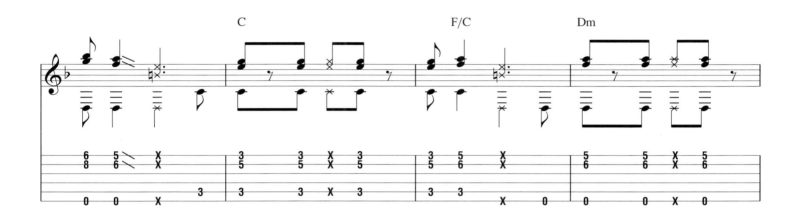

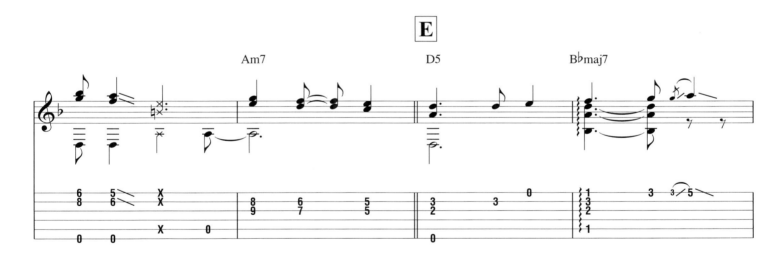

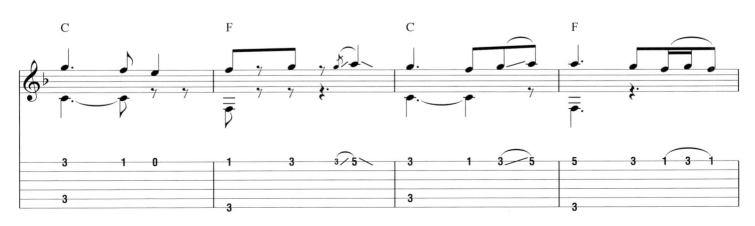

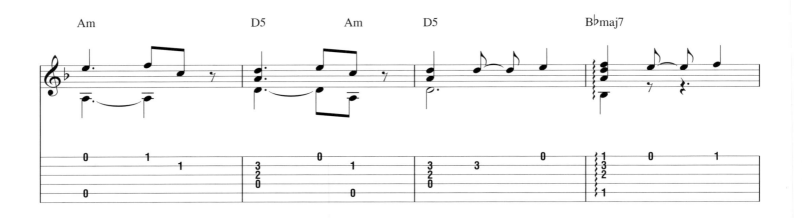

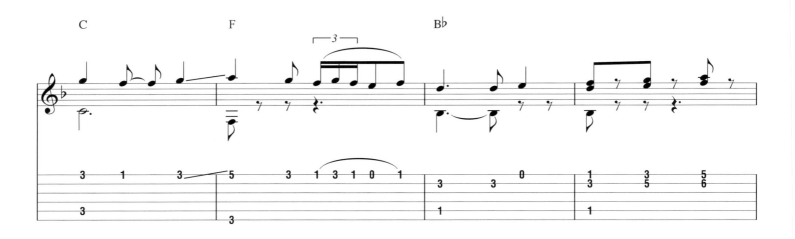

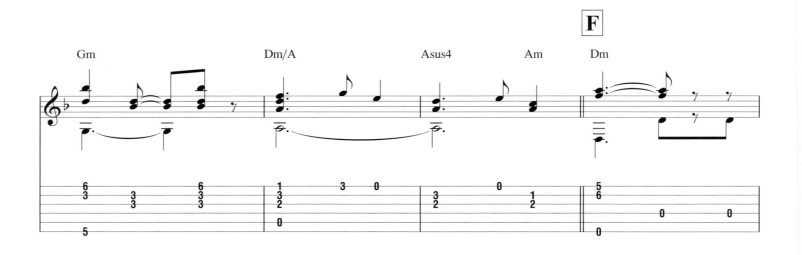

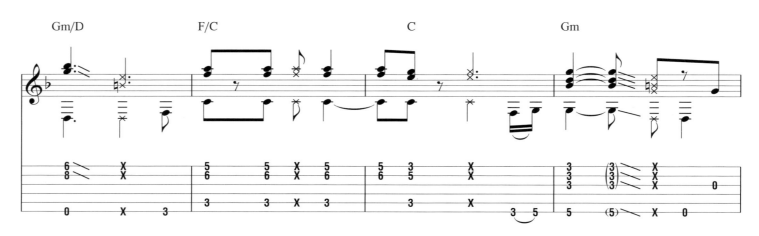

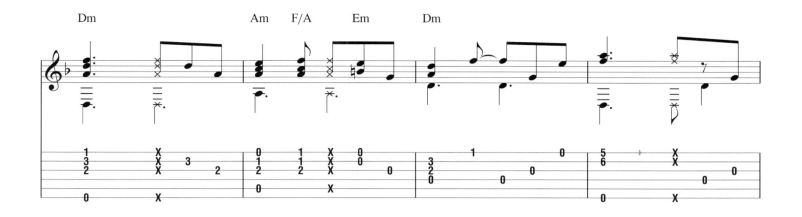

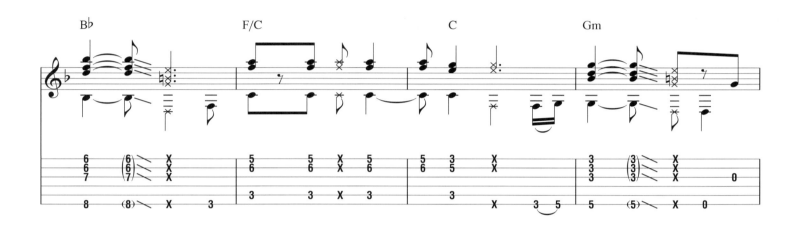

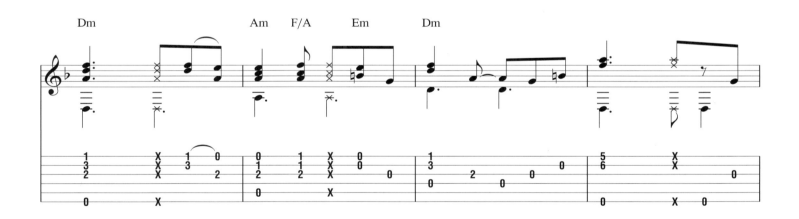

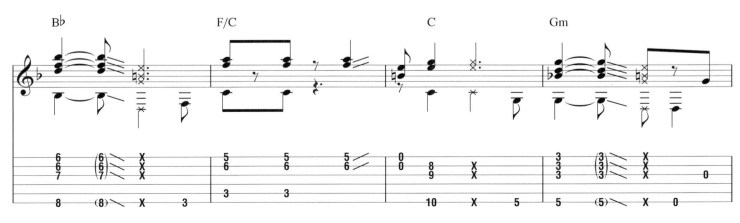

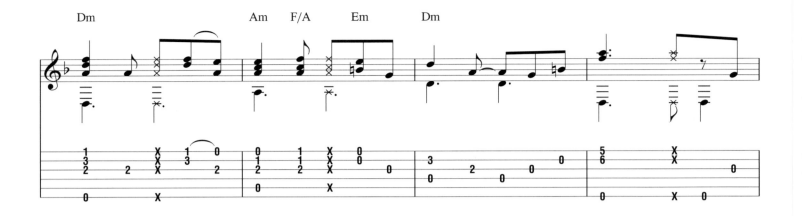

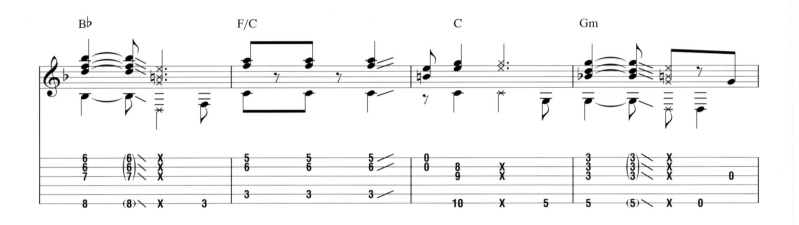

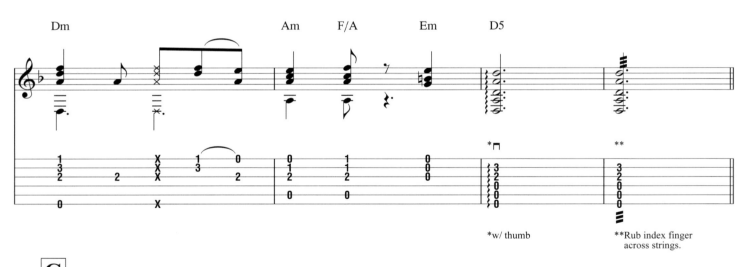

*w/ thumb

**Rub index finger
across strings.

G

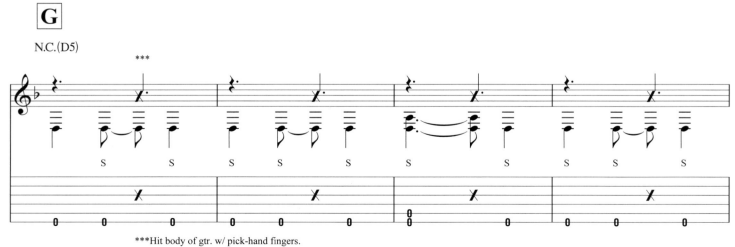

***Hit body of gtr. w/ pick-hand fingers.

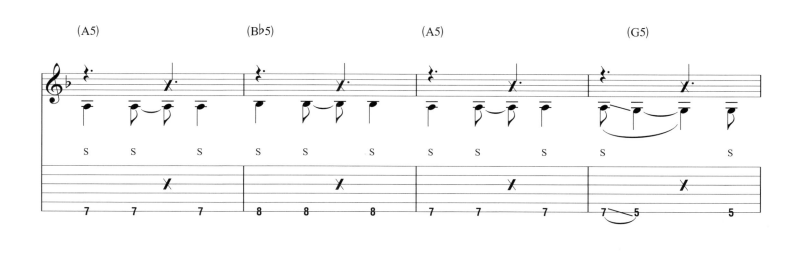

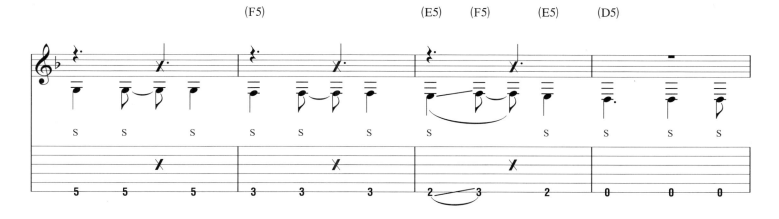

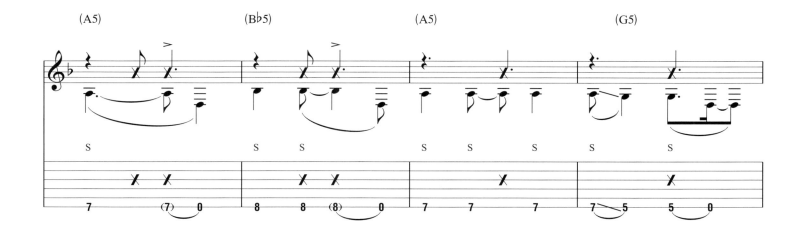

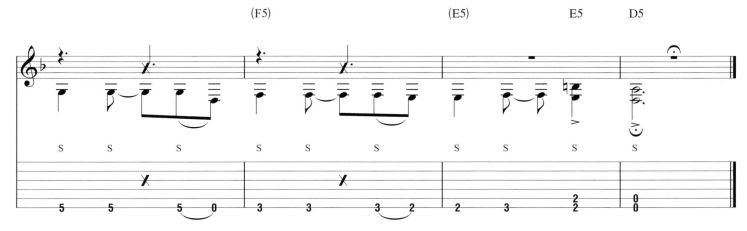

Hello

Words and Music by Adele Adkins and Greg Kurstin

Tune down 1 step, Capo II:
(low to high) D-G-C-F-A-D

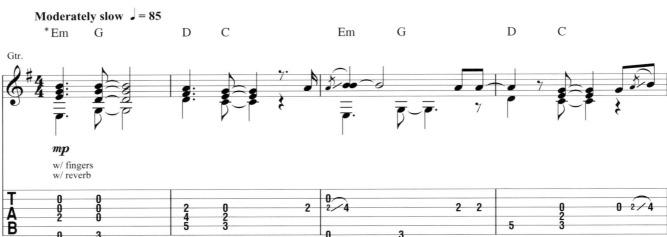

*Chord symbols reflect chord names respective to capoed gtr.
Chord symbols reflect implied harmony.
Capoed fret is "0" in tab.

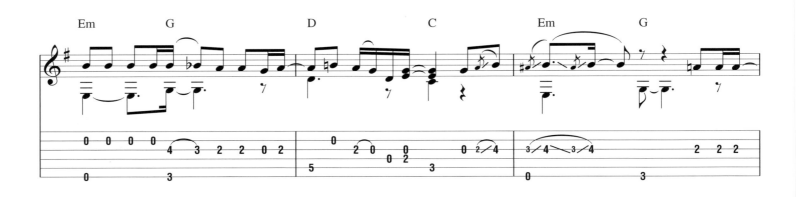

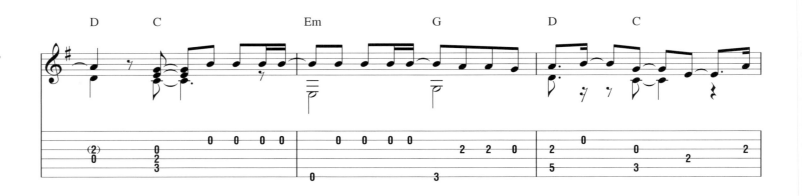

Copyright © 2015 MELTED STONE PUBLISHING LTD., EMI APRIL MUSIC INC. and KURSTIN MUSIC
This arrangement Copyright © 2017 MELTED STONE PUBLISHING LTD., EMI APRIL MUSIC INC. and KURSTIN MUSIC
All Rights for MELTED STONE PUBLISHING LTD. in the U.S. and Canada Administered by
UNIVERSAL - SONGS OF POLYGRAM INTERNATIONAL, INC.
All Rights for EMI APRIL MUSIC INC. and KURSTIN MUSIC Administered by SONY/ATV MUSIC PUBLISHING LLC,
424 Church Street, Suite 1200, Nashville, TN 37219
All Rights Reserved   Used by Permission

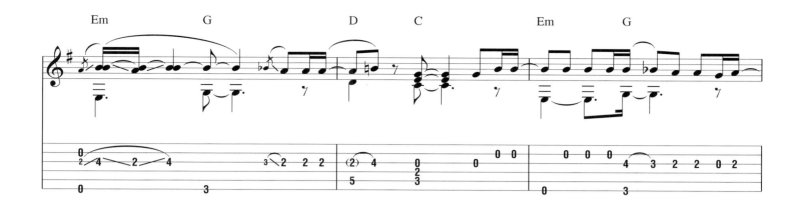

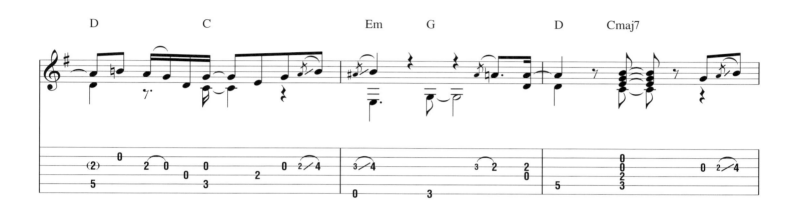

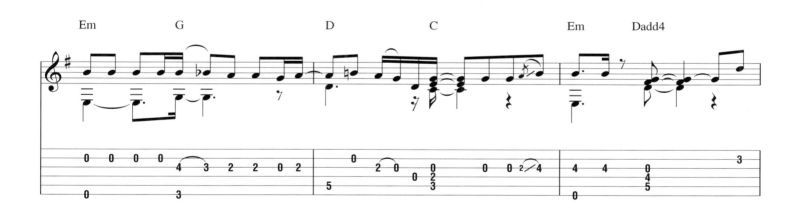

*w/ thumb

B

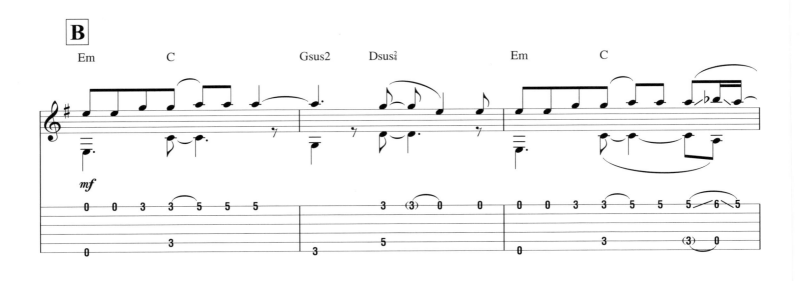

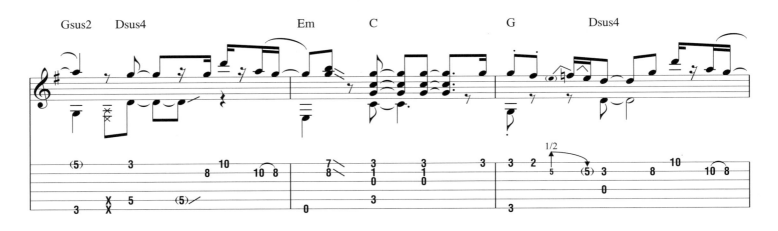

*w/ palm & thumb

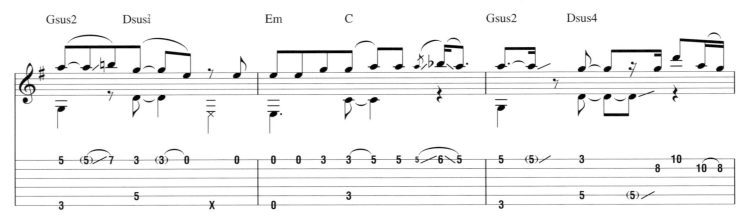

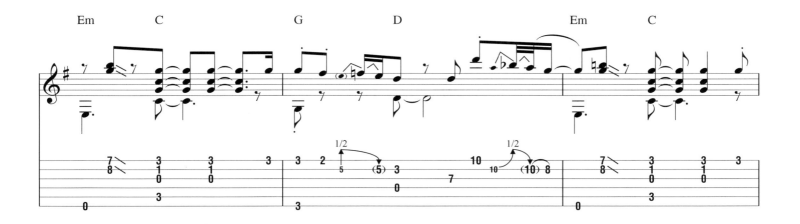

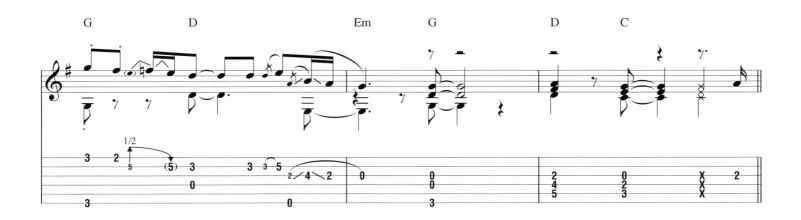

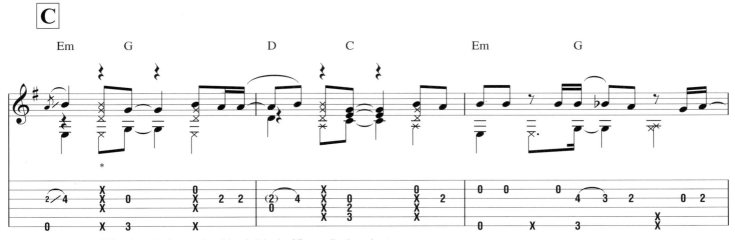

*Hit strings simultaneously w/ thumb & back of fingernails, throughout.

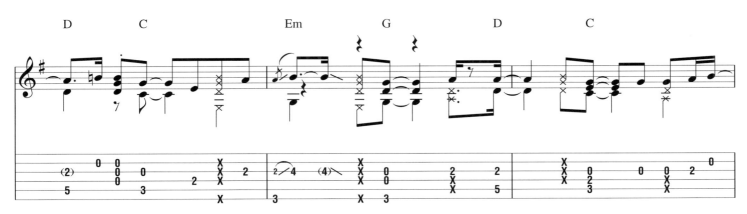

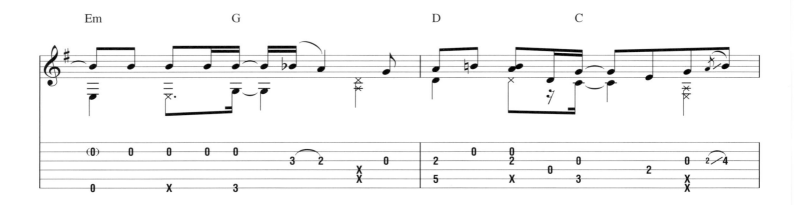

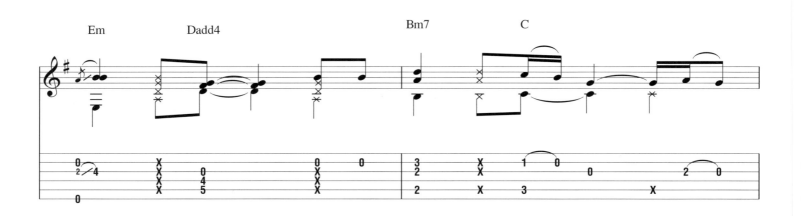

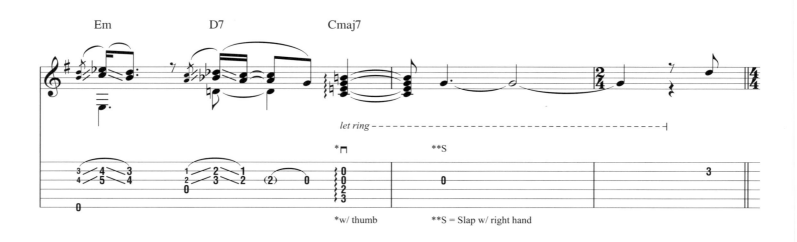

*w/ thumb   **S = Slap w/ right hand

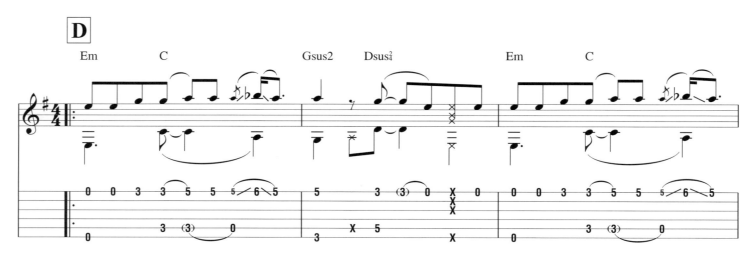

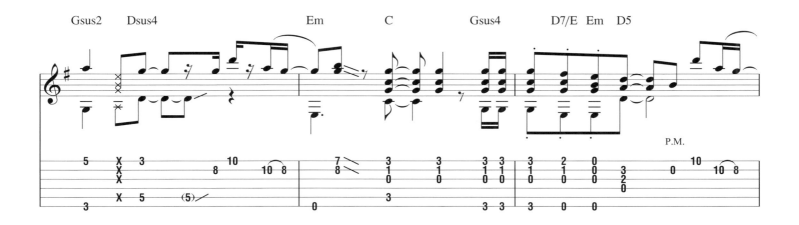

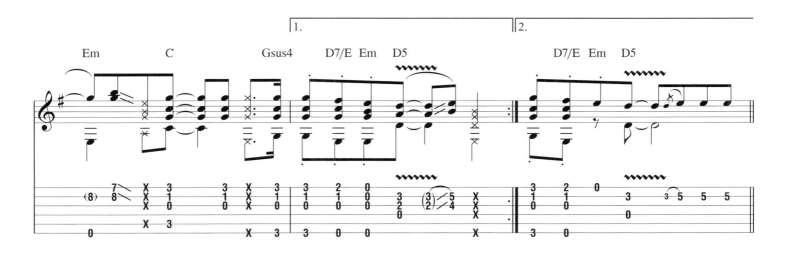

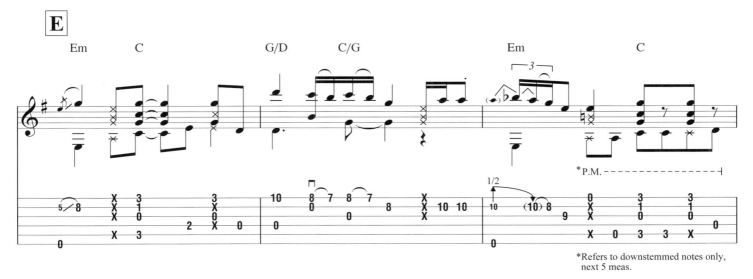

*Refers to downstemmed notes only, next 5 meas.

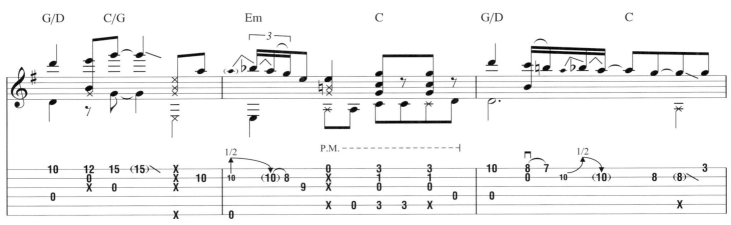

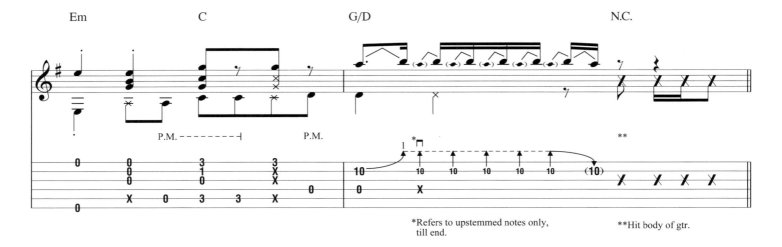

*Refers to upstemmed notes only, till end.

**Hit body of gtr.

F

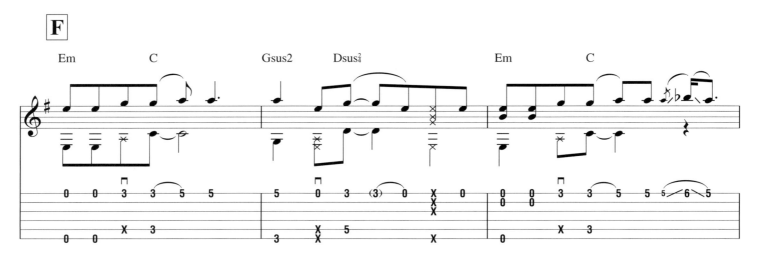

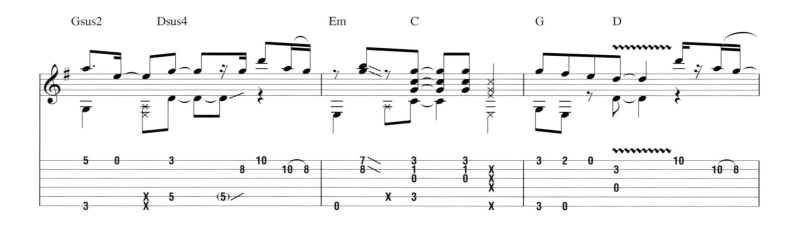

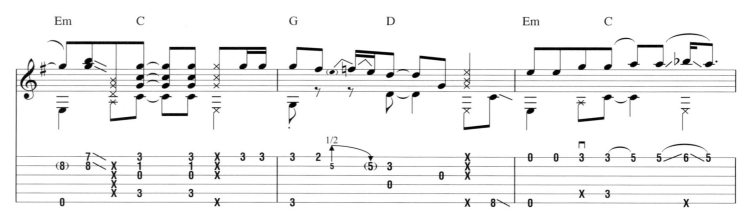

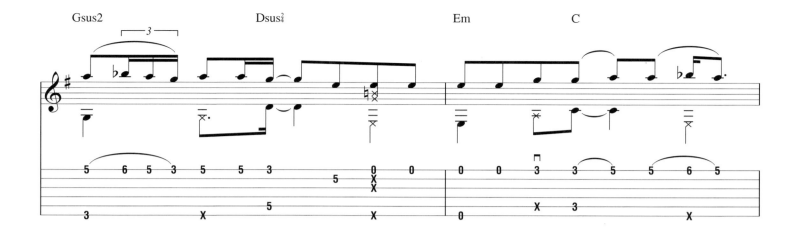

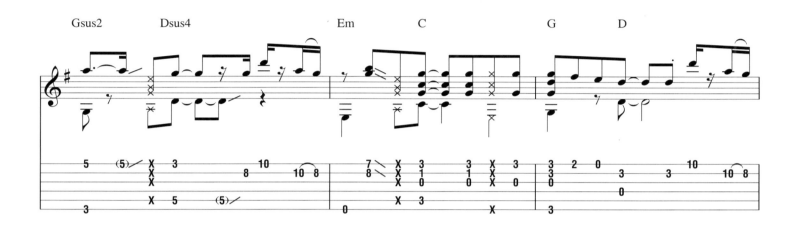

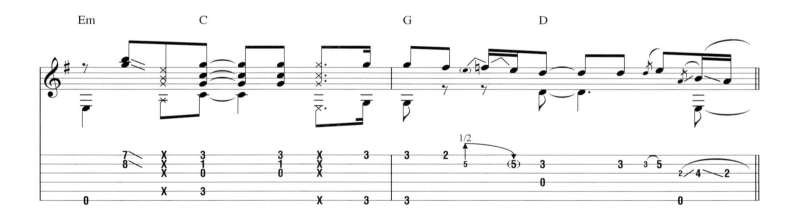

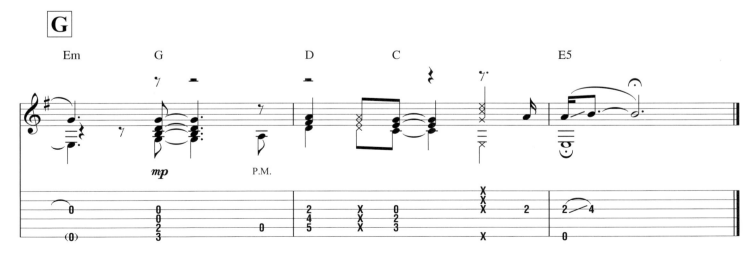

The House of the Rising Sun

Words and Music by Alan Price

Tune down 1 step:
(low to high) D-G-C-F-A-D

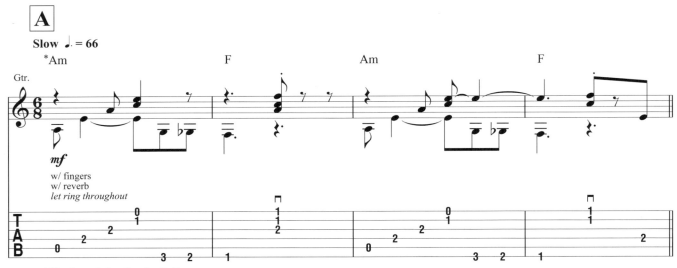

*Chords symbols reflect implied harmony.

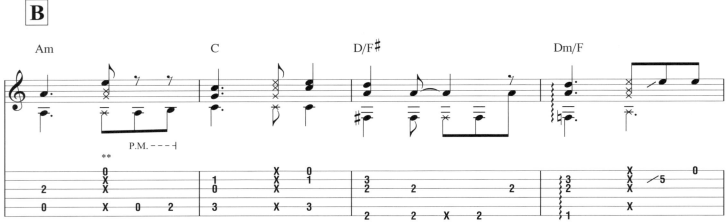

**Hit strings simultaneously w/ thumb,
palm & backs of fingernails, throughout.

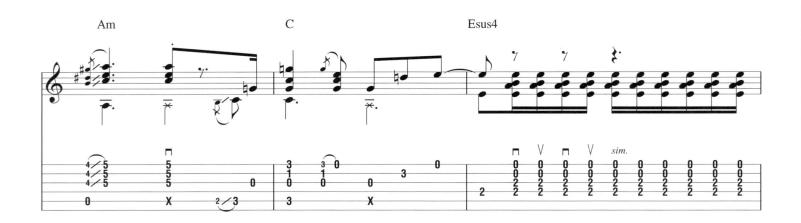

Copyright © 1964 Keith Prowse Music Publishing Co., Ltd. and ole Cantaloupe Music
Copyright Renewed
This arrangement Copyright © 2017 Keith Prowse Music Publishing Co., Ltd. and ole Cantaloupe Music
All Rights Administered by Sony/ATV Music Publishing LLC, 424 Church Street, Suite 1200, Nashville, TN 37219
International Copyright Secured   All Rights Reserved

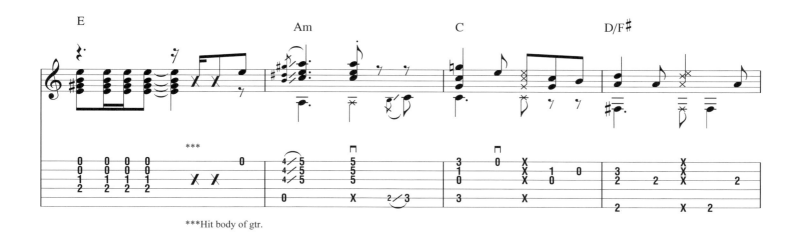

***Hit body of gtr.

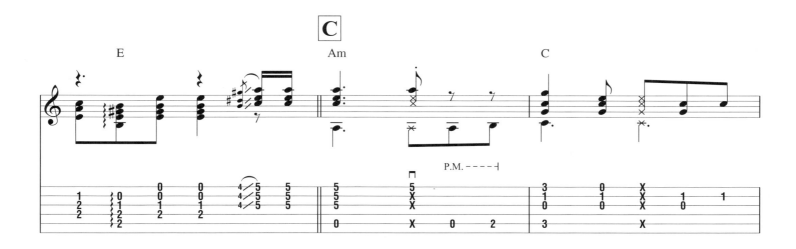

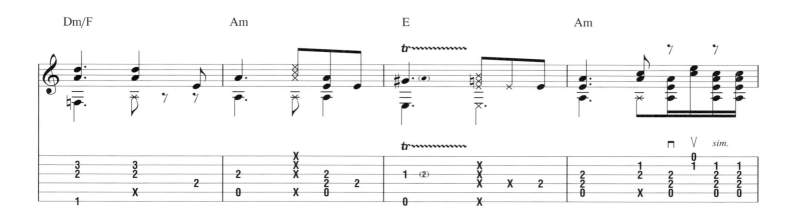

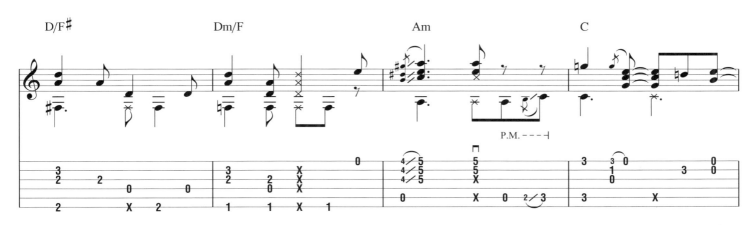

Esus4

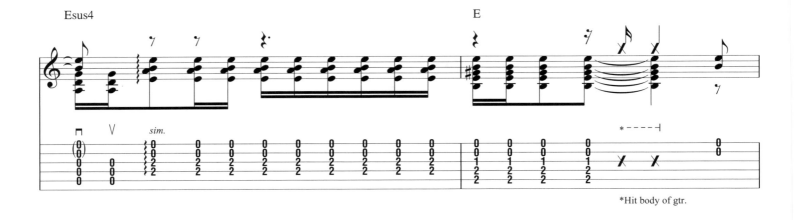

E

*Hit body of gtr.

Am   C   D/F#   Dm/F

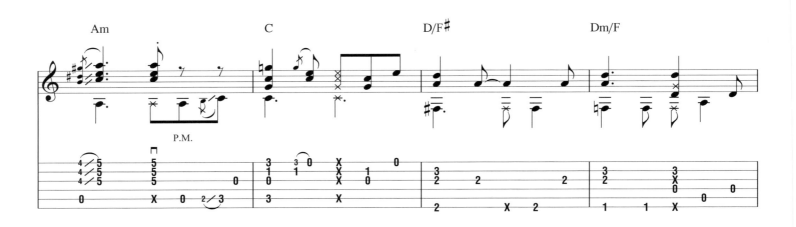

P.M.

Am   E   Am   E

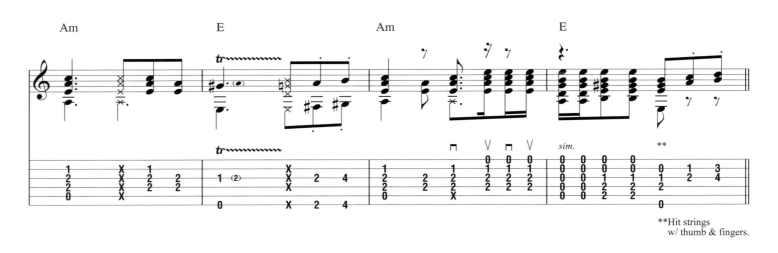

**Hit strings
w/ thumb & fingers.

D

Am   Abm7   Gm7   C   D/F#   Dm/F

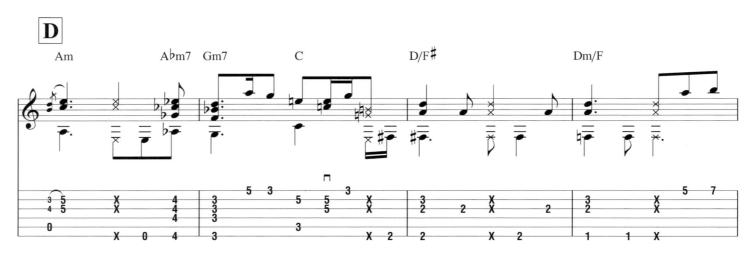

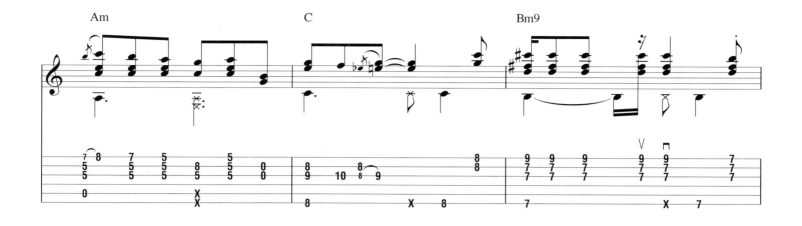

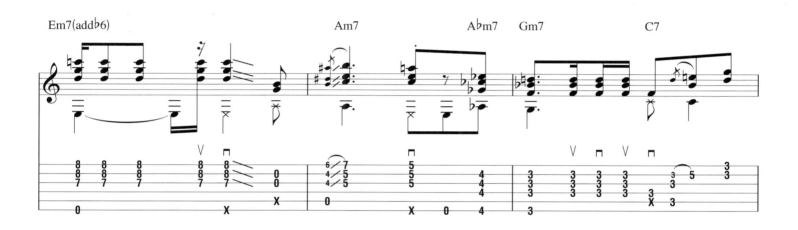

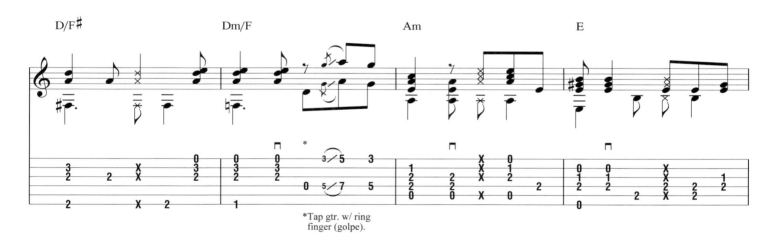

*Tap gtr. w/ ring
finger (golpe).

E

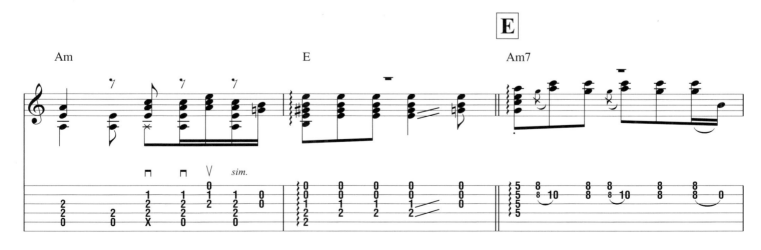

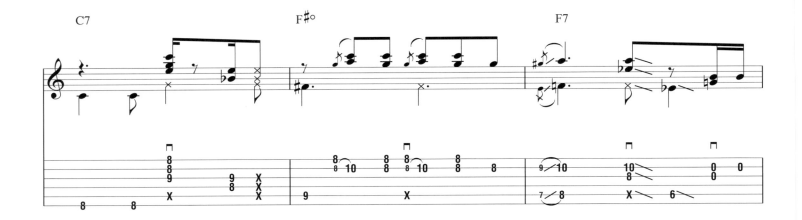

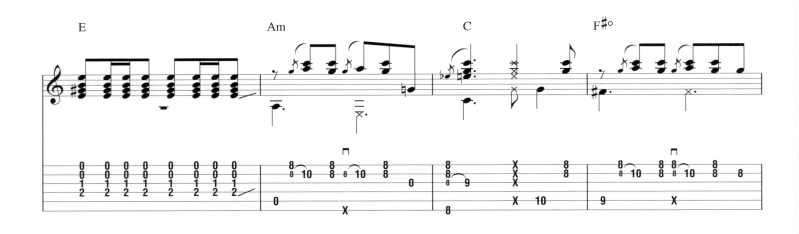

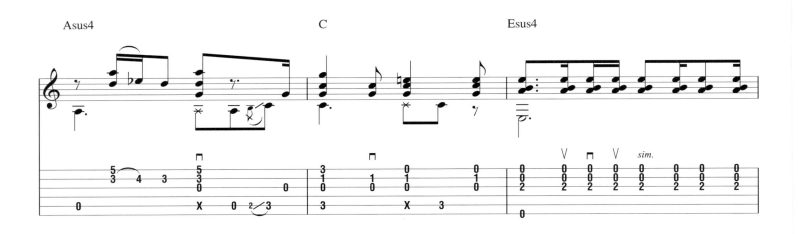

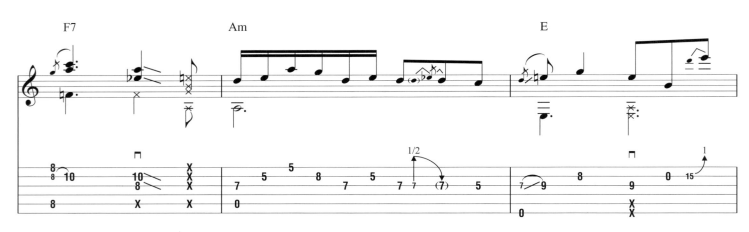

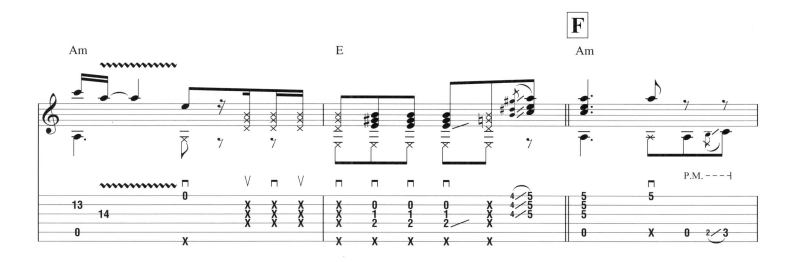

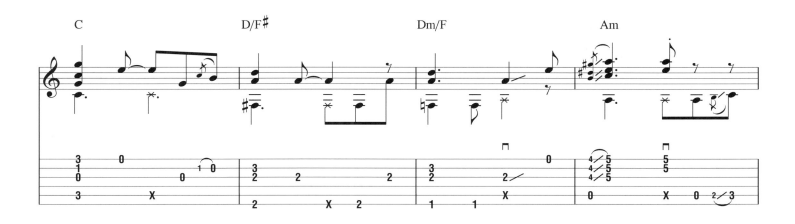

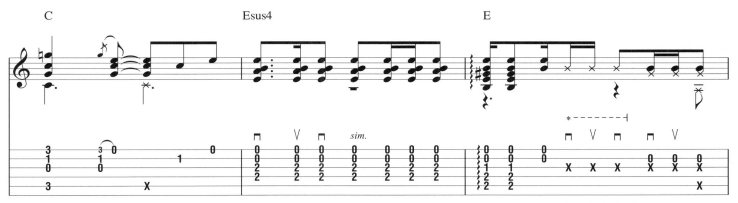

*Scratch body of gtr.
w/ strumming motion.

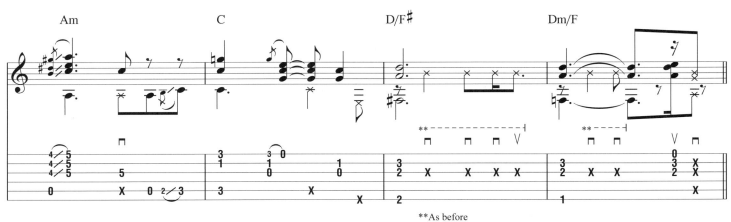

**As before

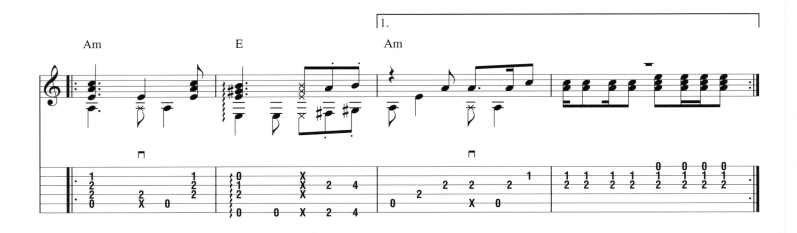

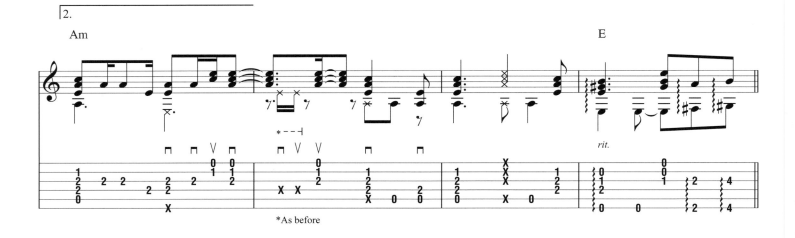

G

A tempo

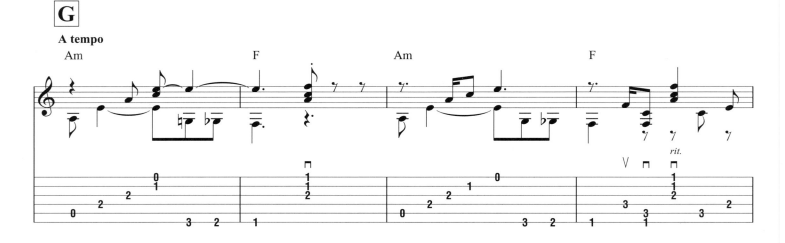

Free time

*As before

**Continuous rasgueado

***Rub index fingertip
across strings.

Listen to Your Heart

Words and Music by Per Gessle and Mats Persson

Tune down 1 step:
(low to high) D-G-C-F-A-D

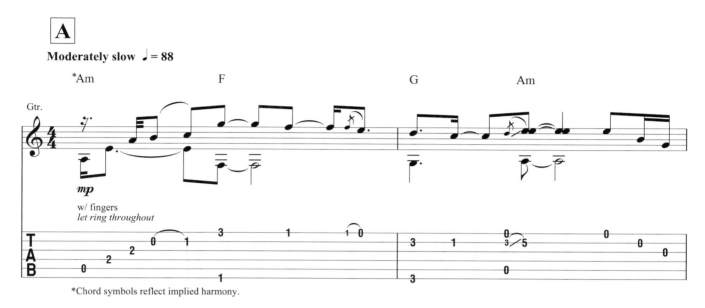

*Chord symbols reflect implied harmony.

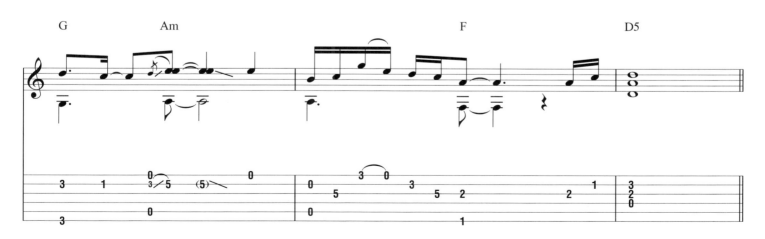

Copyright © 1988, 1989 Jimmy Fun Music AB
This arrangement Copyright © 2017 Jimmy Fun Music AB
All Rights Administered by Songs Of Kobalt Music Publishing
All Rights Reserved   Used by Permission

B

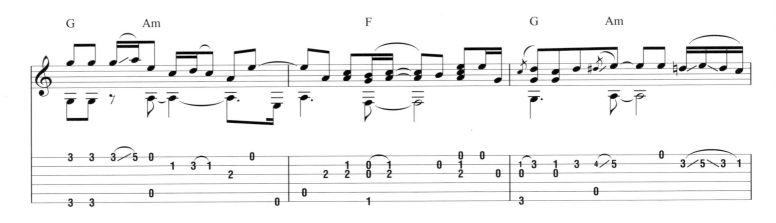

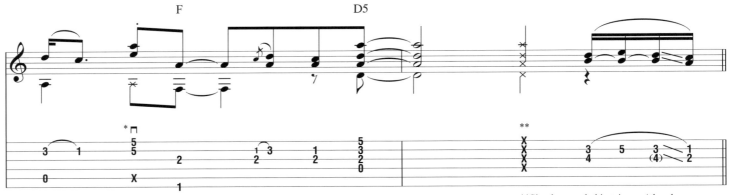

*In a single downstroke, sound upstemmed notes by striking strings w/ backs of fingernails while slapping thumb against strings to produce a percussive sound (downstemmed notes), throughout.

**Simultaneously hit strings w/ thumb & backs of fingernails to produce a percussive sound, throughout.

C

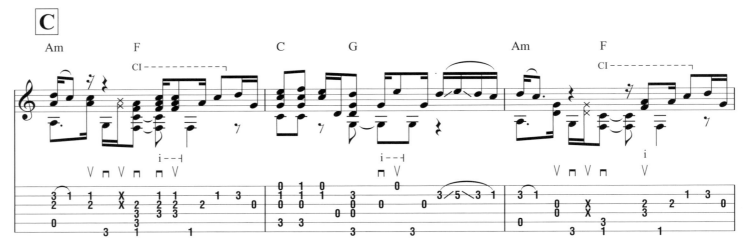

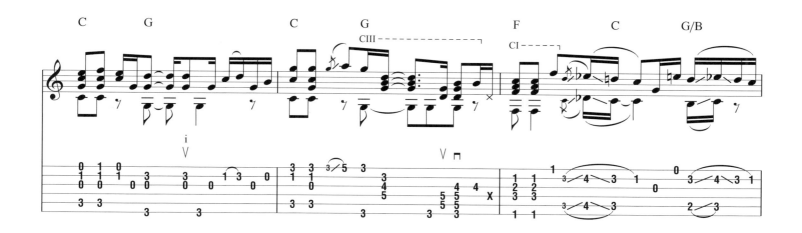

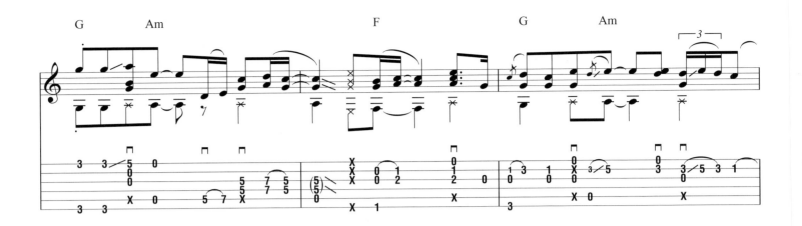

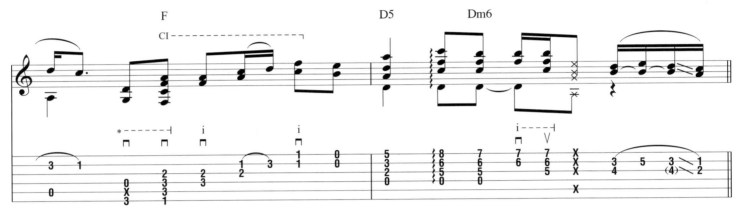

*Strum w/ index finger as if holding a pick.

E

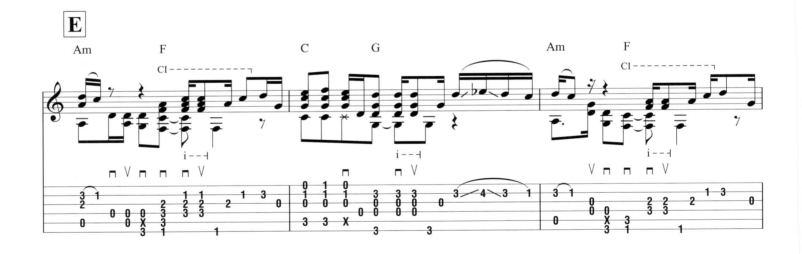

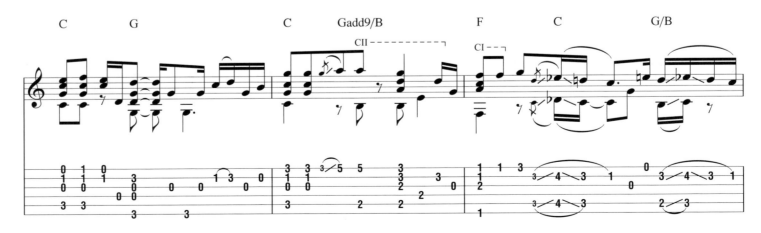

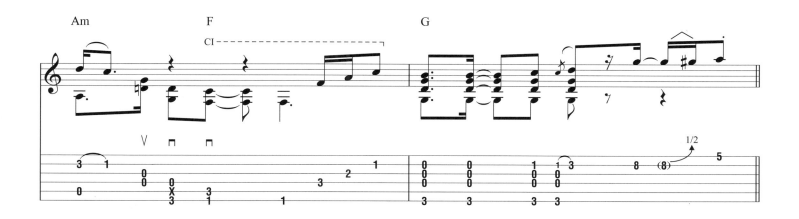

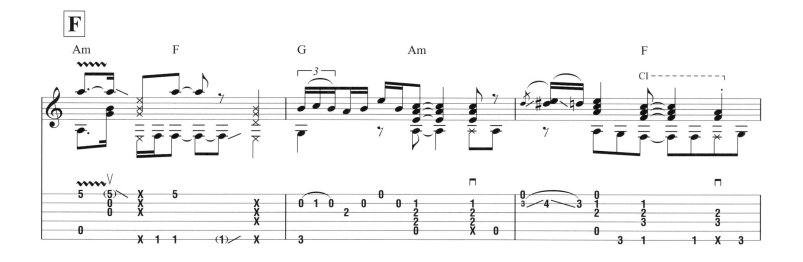

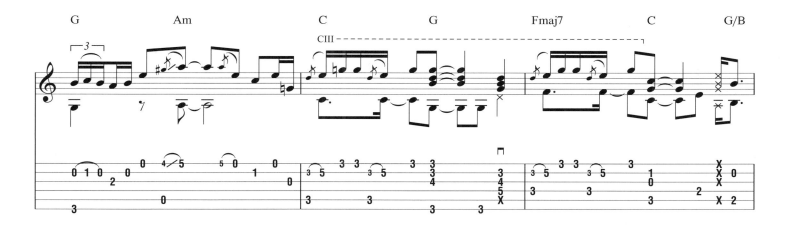

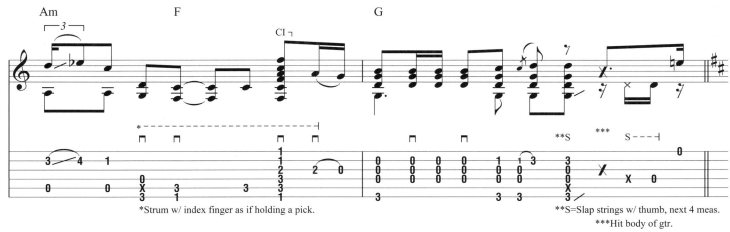

*Strum w/ index finger as if holding a pick.

**S=Slap strings w/ thumb, next 4 meas.

***Hit body of gtr.

G

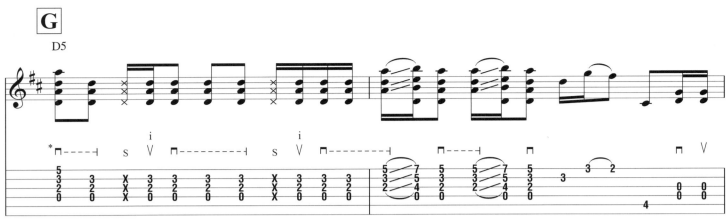

*Strum w/ index finger as if holding a pick, next 8 meas.

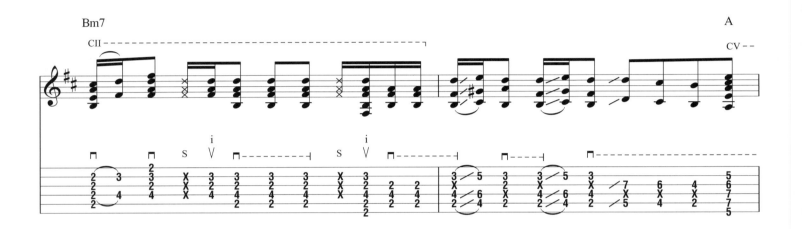

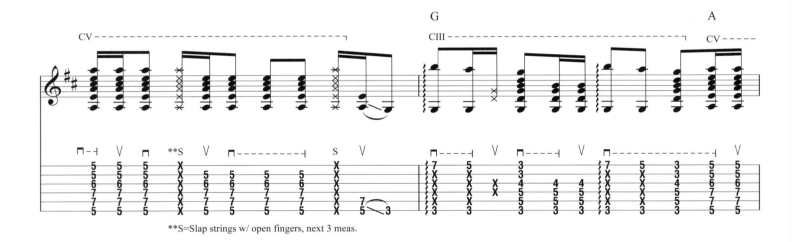

**S=Slap strings w/ open fingers, next 3 meas.

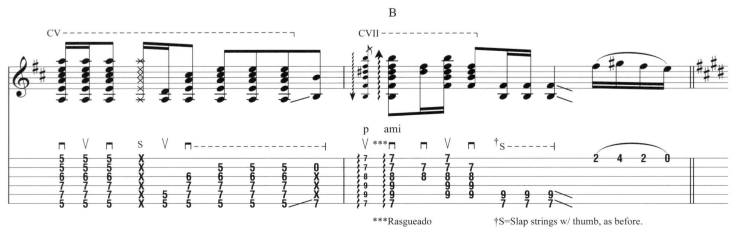

***Rasgueado   †S=Slap strings w/ thumb, as before.

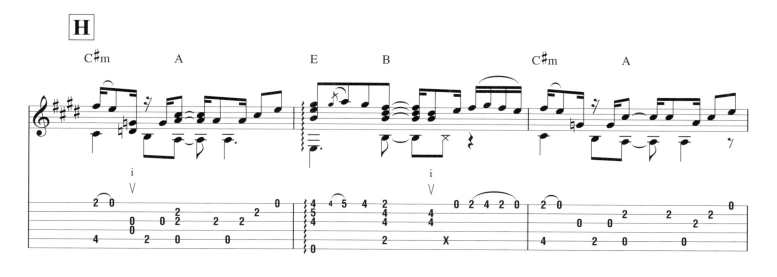

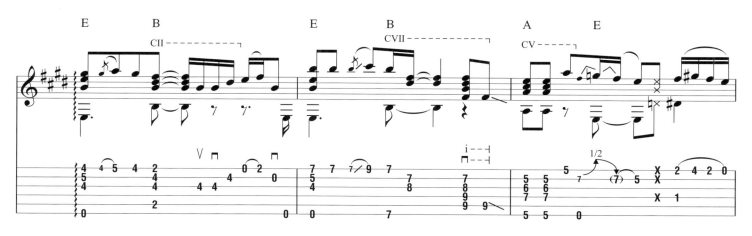

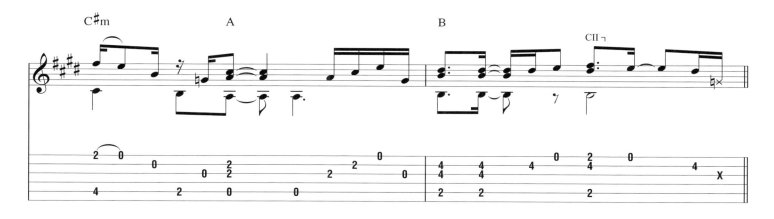

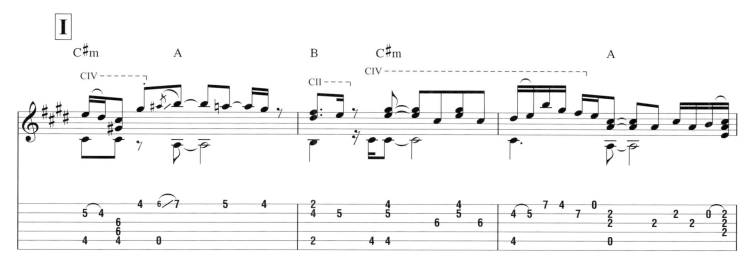

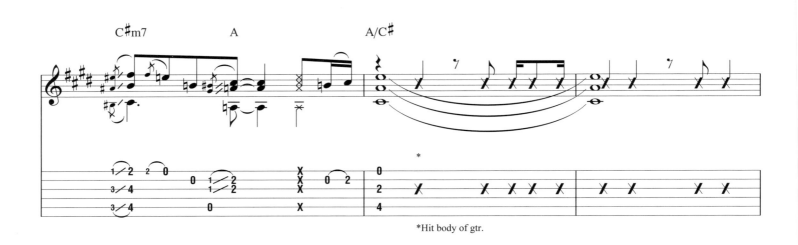

*Hit body of gtr.

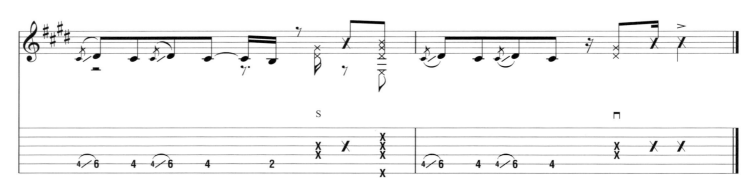

Lonely Day

Words and Music by Daron Malakian and Serj Tankian

Drop D tuning, down 1 step:
(low to high) C-G-C-F-A-D

*Chord symbols reflect implied harmony.

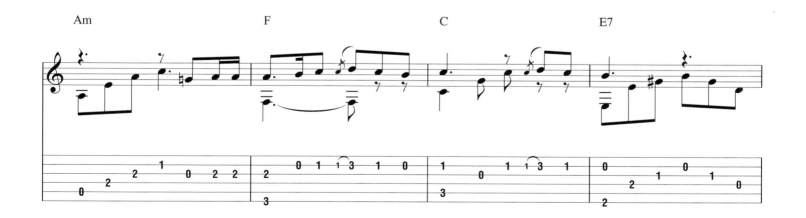

Copyright © 2005 Sony/ATV Music Publishing LLC, Malakian Publishing and Stunning Suppository Songs
This arrangement Copyright © 2017 Sony/ATV Music Publishing LLC, Malakian Publishing and Stunning Suppository Songs
All Rights Administered by Sony/ATV Music Publishing LLC, 424 Church Street, Suite 1200, Nashville, TN 37219
International Copyright Secured   All Rights Reserved

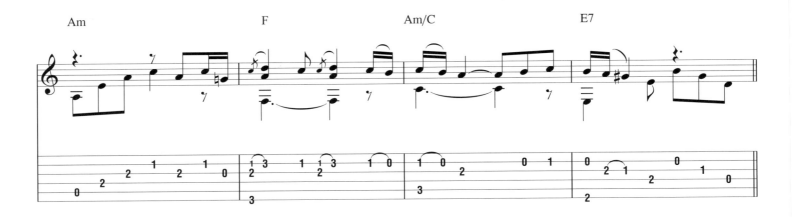

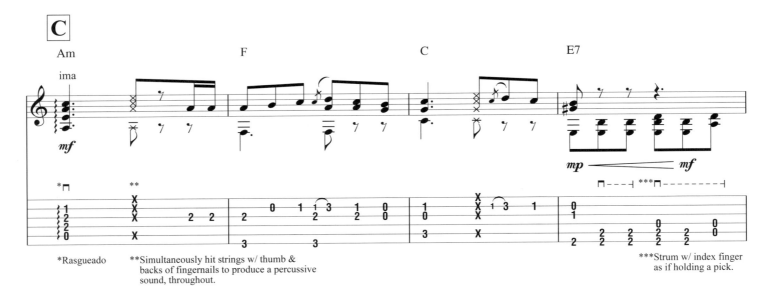

*Rasgueado   **Simultaneously hit strings w/ thumb &
backs of fingernails to produce a percussive
sound, throughout.

***Strum w/ index finger
as if holding a pick.

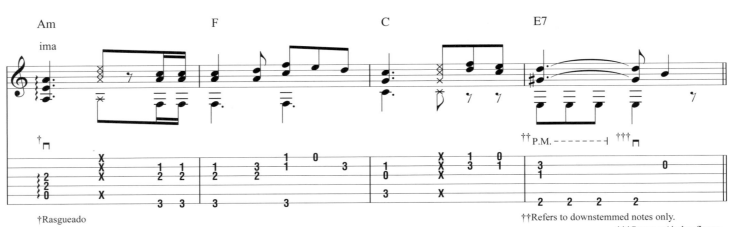

†Rasgueado

††Refers to downstemmed notes only.

†††Strum w/ index finger
as if holding a pick.

D

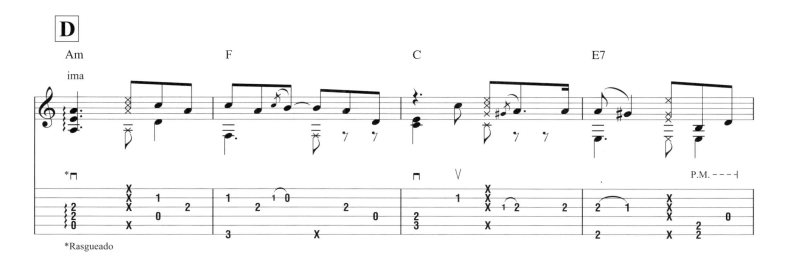

*Rasgueado

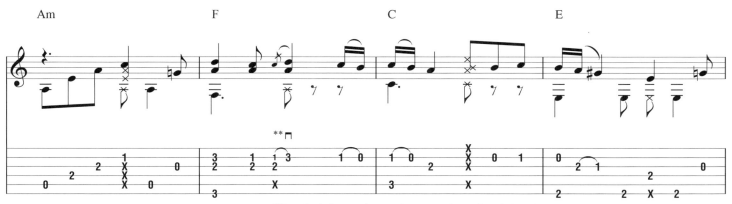

**In a single downstroke, sound upstemmed notes by striking strings
  w/ backs of fingernails while slapping thumb against strings to produce
  a percussive sound (downstemmed notes), throughout.

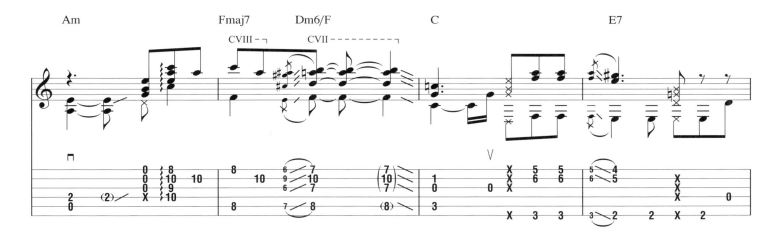

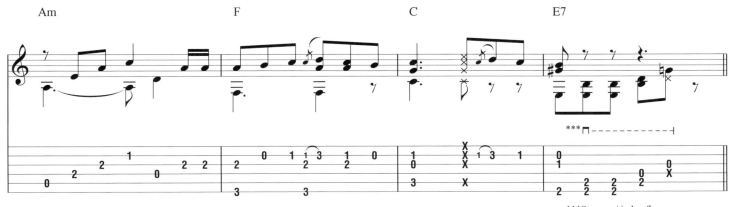

***Strum w/ index finger
   as if holding a pick.

E

F5   E5   G5   Am

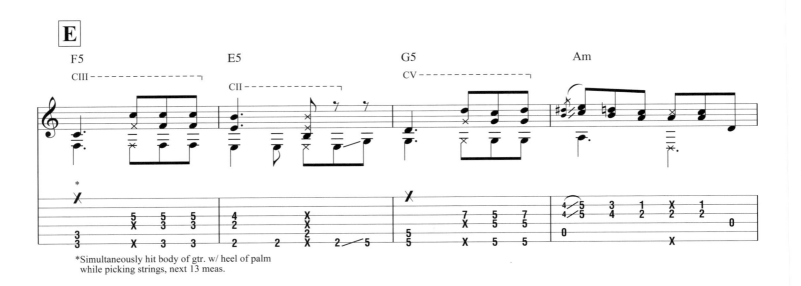

*Simultaneously hit body of gtr. w/ heel of palm
  while picking strings, next 13 meas.

Fmaj7(no3rd)   E7(no3rd)   G5   Am

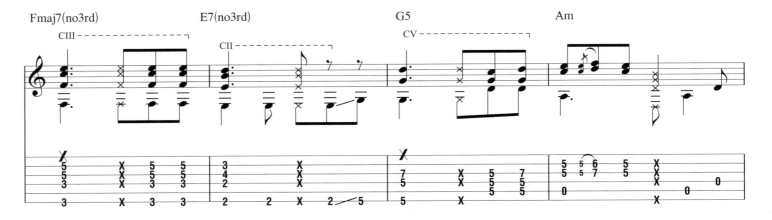

Fmaj7(no3rd)   E7(no3rd)

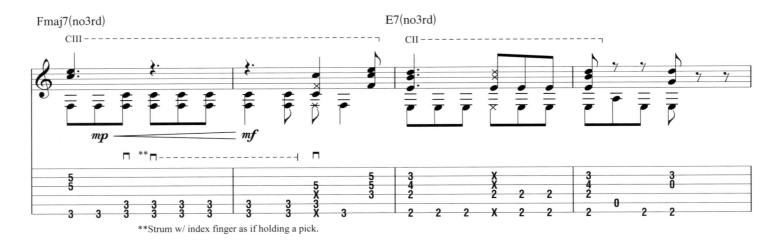

**Strum w/ index finger as if holding a pick.

Am   F   C   E7

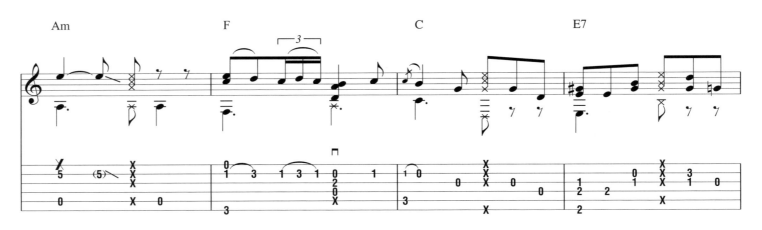

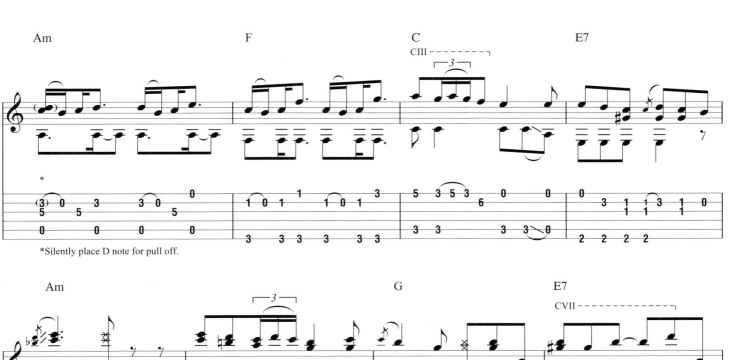

*Silently place D note for pull off.

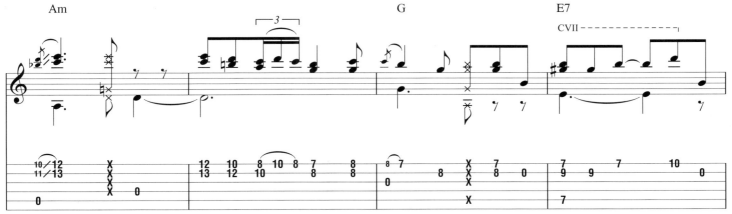

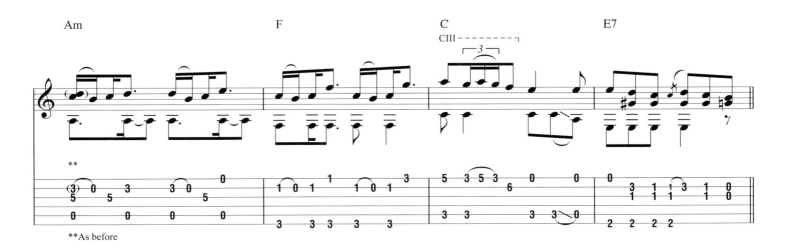

**As before

F

***Strum w/ index finger
as if holding a pick.

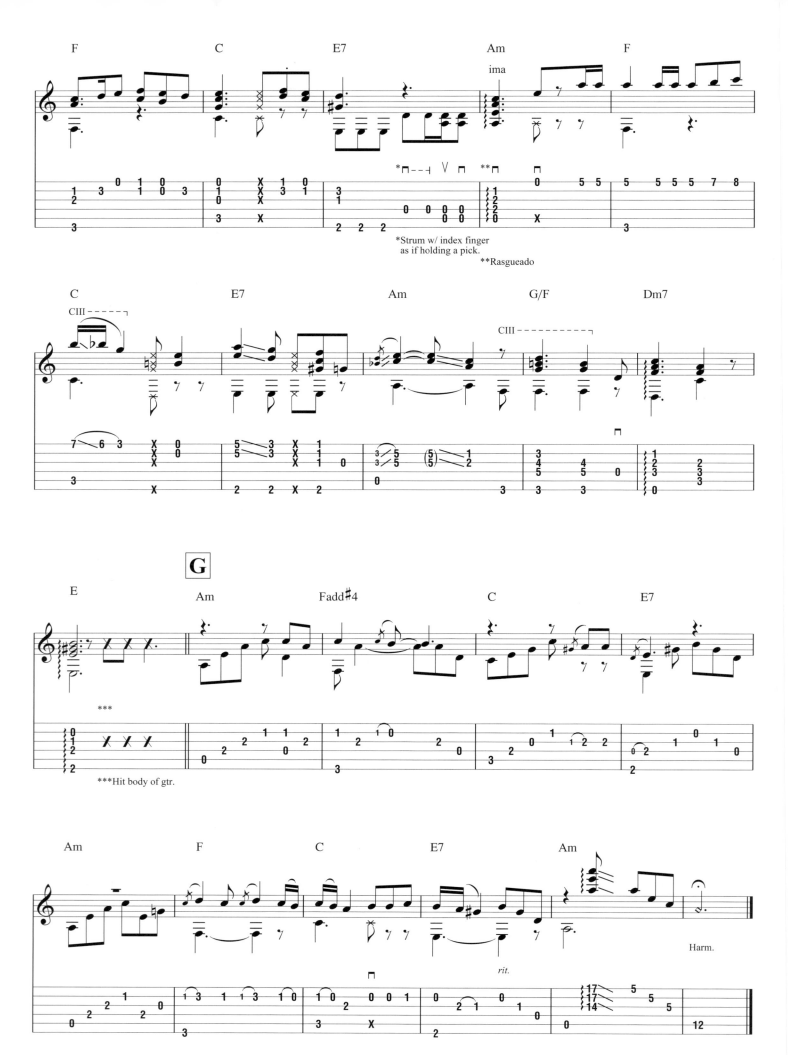

*Strum w/ index finger
as if holding a pick.

**Rasgueado

***Hit body of gtr.

Nothing Else Matters

Words and Music by James Hetfield and Lars Ulrich

Tune down 1 step:
(low to high) D-G-C-F-A-D

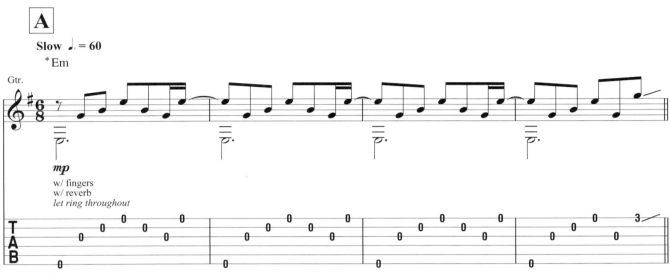

*Chord symbols reflect implied harmony.

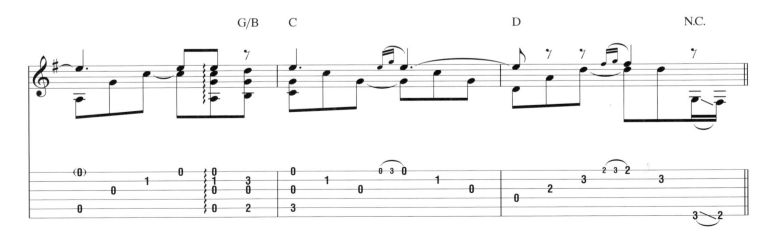

Copyright © 1991 Creeping Death Music (ASCAP)
This arrangement Copyright © 2017 Creeping Death Music (ASCAP)
International Copyright Secured   All Rights Reserved

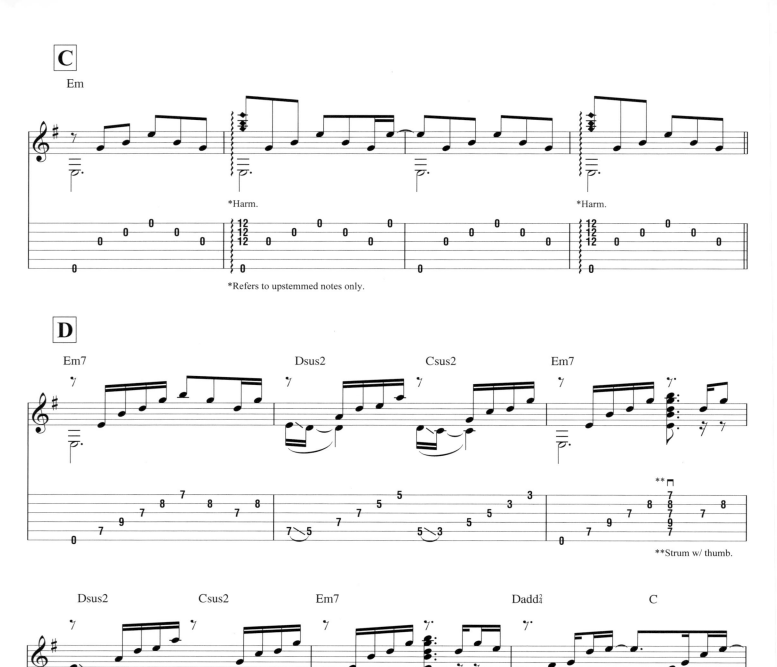

*Refers to upstemmed notes only.

**Strum w/ thumb.

***As before

†As before

E

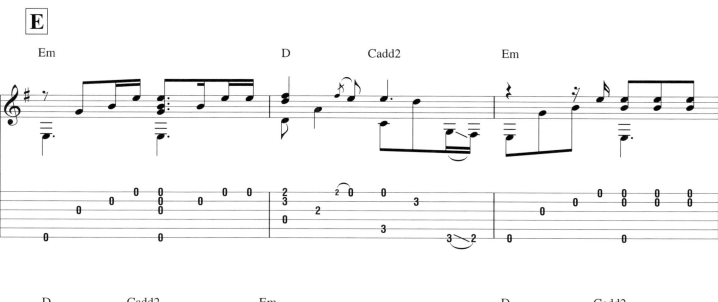

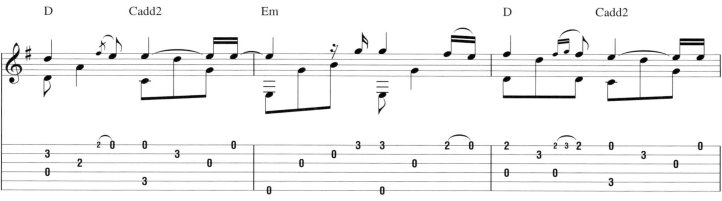

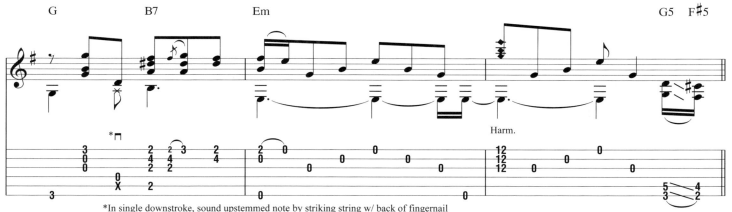

*In single downstroke, sound upstemmed note by striking string w/ back of fingernail
while slapping thumb against strings to produce a percussive sound (downstemmed notes).

F

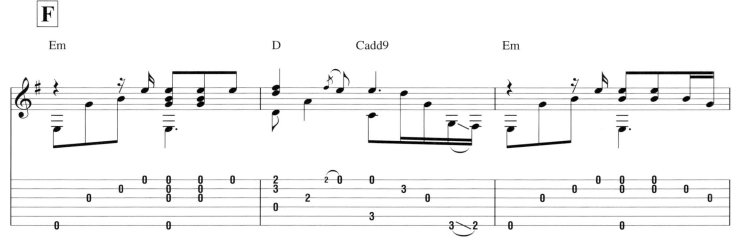

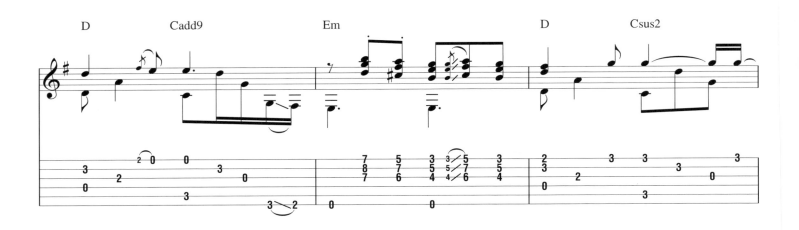

*Simultaneously hit strings w/ thumb & backs
of fingernails to produce a percussive sound.

G

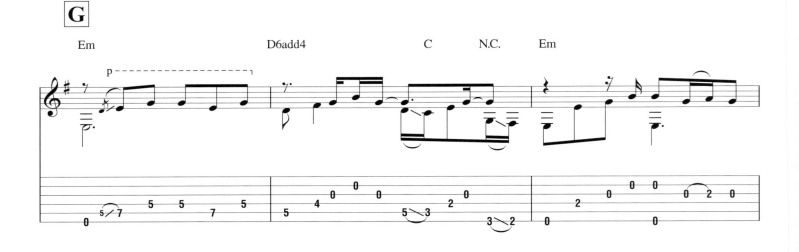

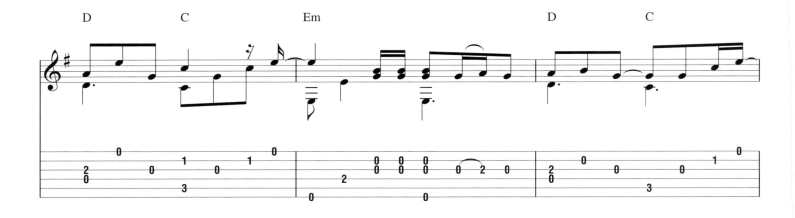

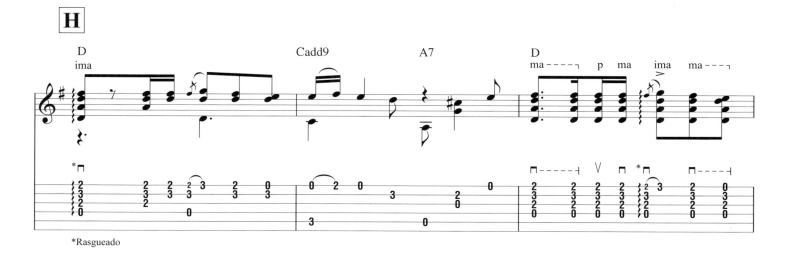

*Rasgueado

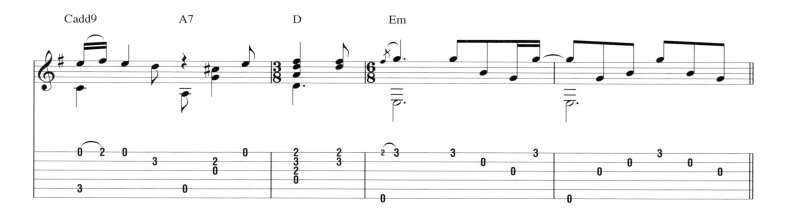

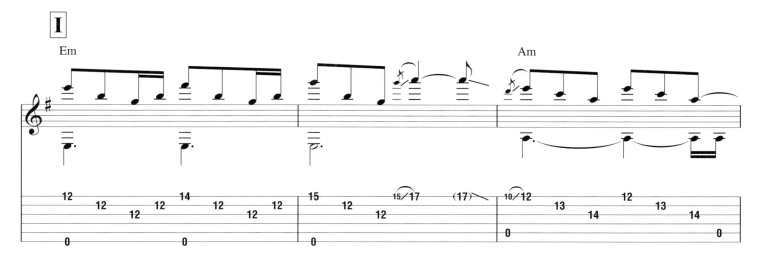

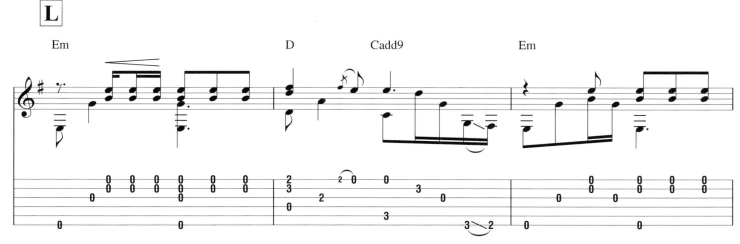

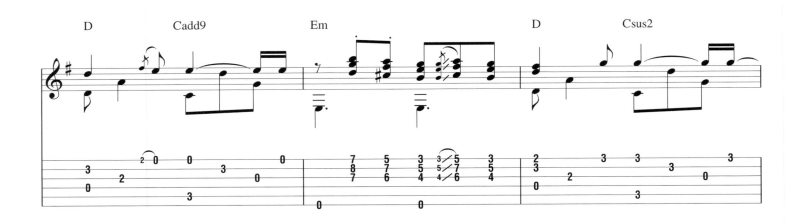

M

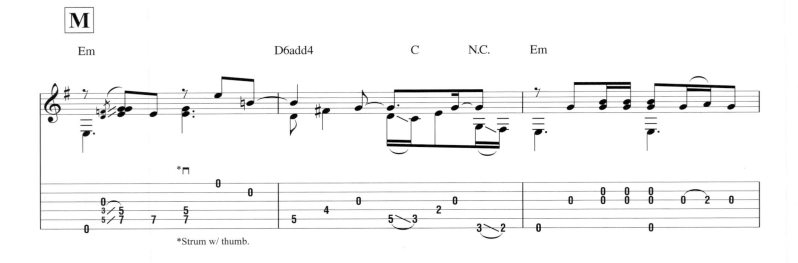

*Strum w/ thumb.

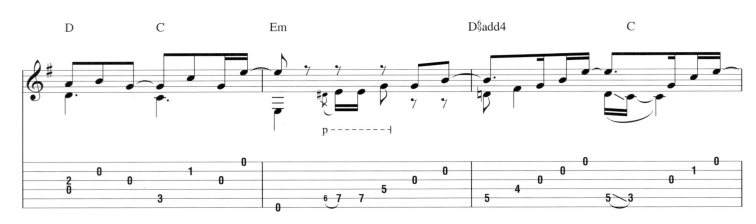

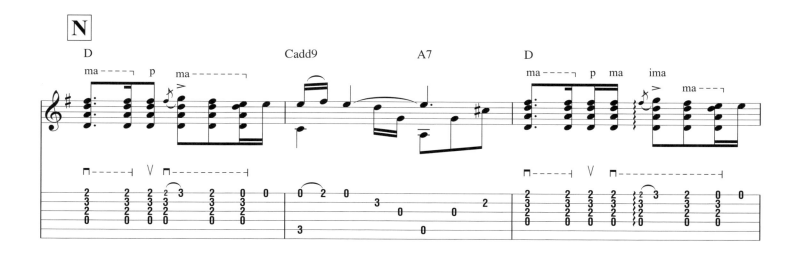

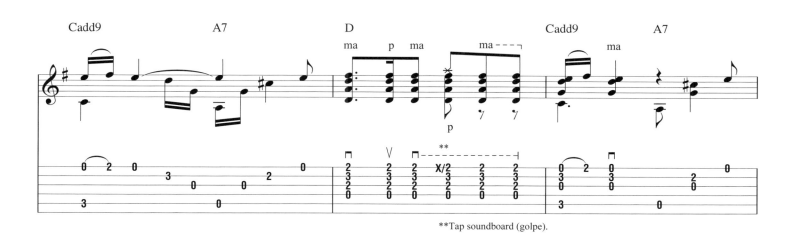

**Tap soundboard (golpe).

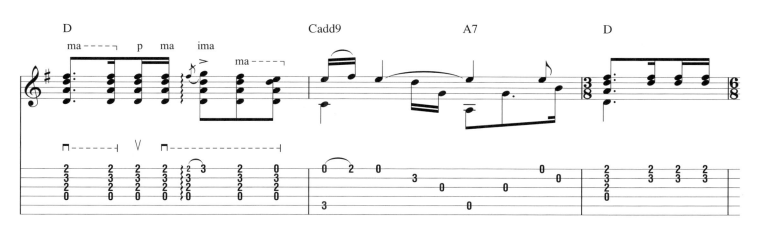

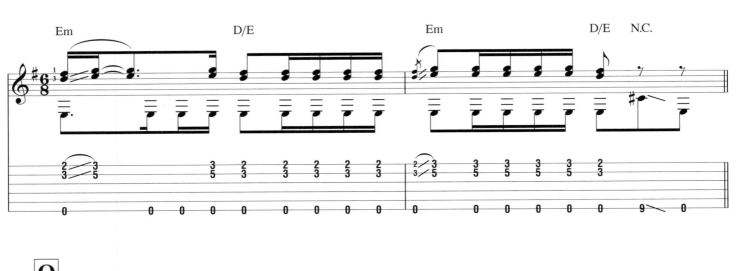

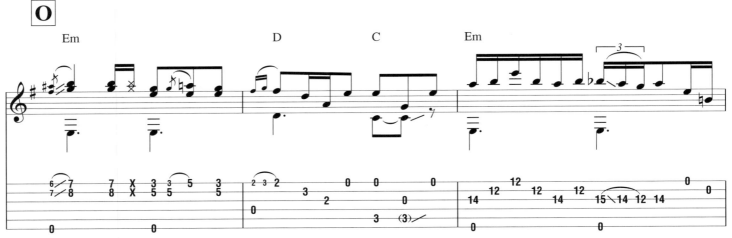

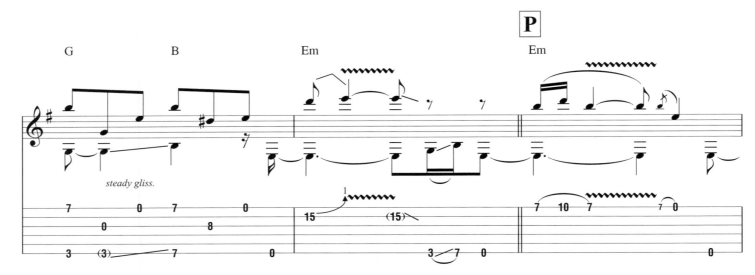

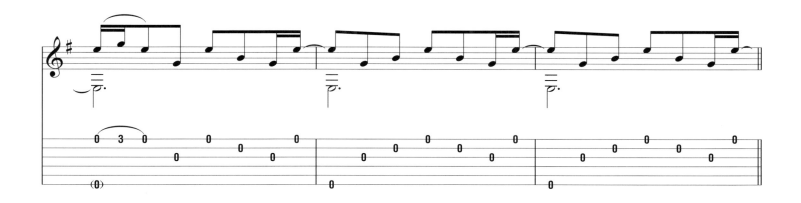

Q

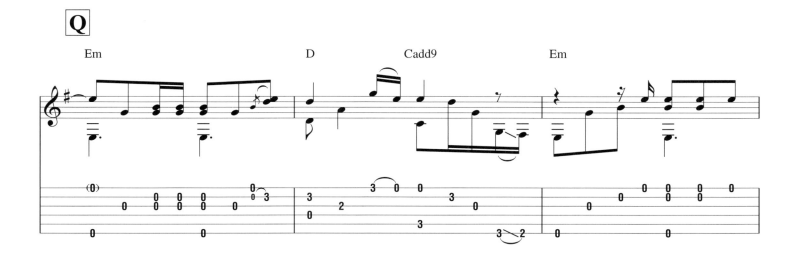

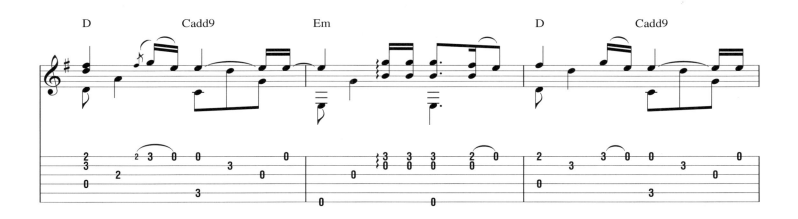

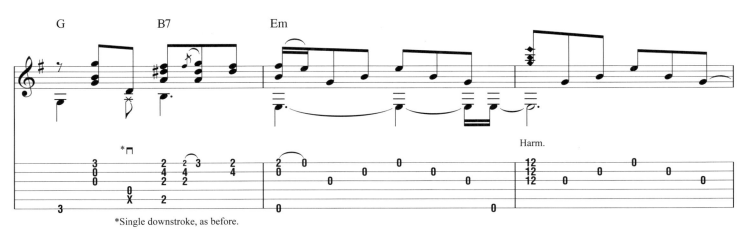

*Single downstroke, as before.

*Refers to upstemmed
notes only.

Numb

Words and Music by Chester Bennington, Rob Bourdon, Brad Delson, Joe Hahn, Mike Shinoda and Dave Farrell

Drop C tuning, down 1 1/2 steps:
(low to high) A-F#-B-E-G#-C#

Moderately ♩ = 120

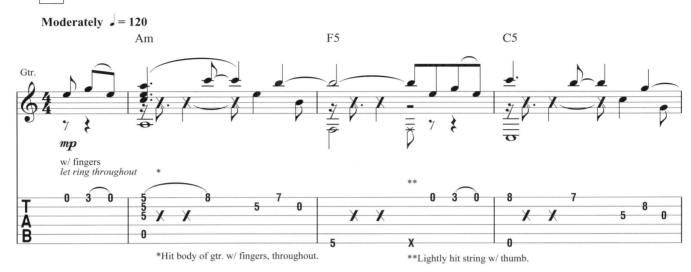

*Hit body of gtr. w/ fingers, throughout.   **Lightly hit string w/ thumb.

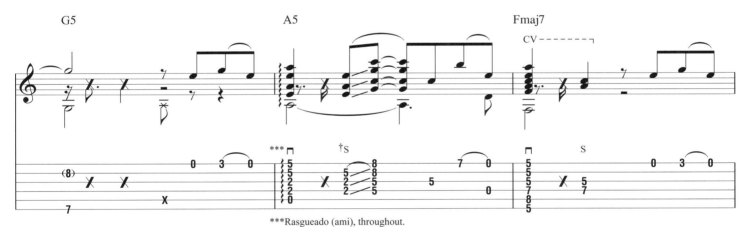

***Rasgueado (ami), throughout.
†S=Slap strings w/ thumb, throughout.

Copyright © 2003 by Universal Music - Z Songs, Chesterchaz Publishing, Rob Bourdon Music,
Nondisclosure Agreement Music, Big Bad Mr. Hahn Music, Kenji Kobayashi Music and Pancakey Cakes Music
This arrangement Copyright © 2017 by Universal Music - Z Songs, Chesterchaz Publishing, Rob Bourdon Music,
Nondisclosure Agreement Music, Big Bad Mr. Hahn Music, Kenji Kobayashi Music and Pancakey Cakes Music
All Rights in the U.S. Administered by Universal Music - Z Songs
International Copyright Secured   All Rights Reserved

*Simultaneously hit strings w/ thumb & backs of fingernails to produce a percussive sound, throughout.

**In a single downstroke, sound upstemmed notes by striking strings w/ backs of fingernails while slapping thumb against lower string to produce a percussive sound (downstemmed notes), throughout.

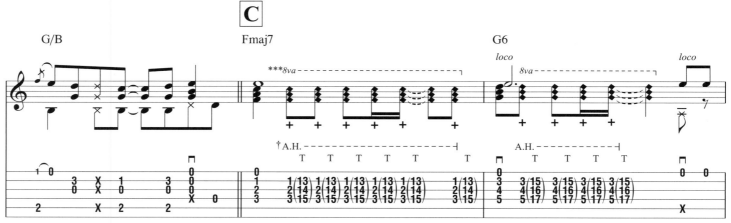

C

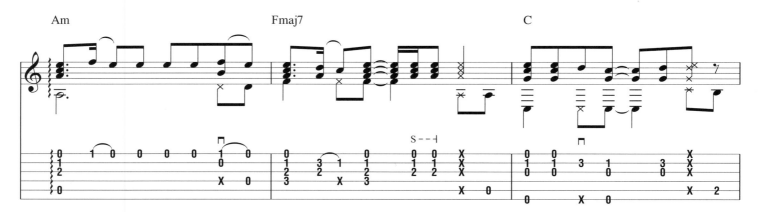

***Refers to downstemmed notes only, next 2 meas.
†Artificial harmonics produced by tapping strings 12 frets above fretted notes.

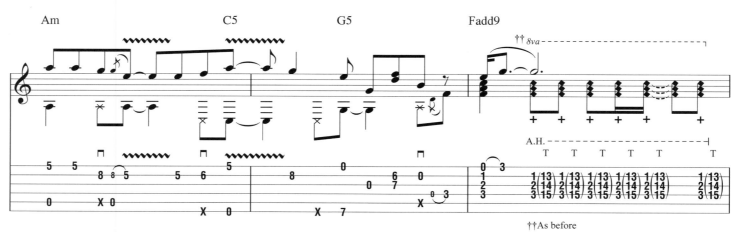

††As before

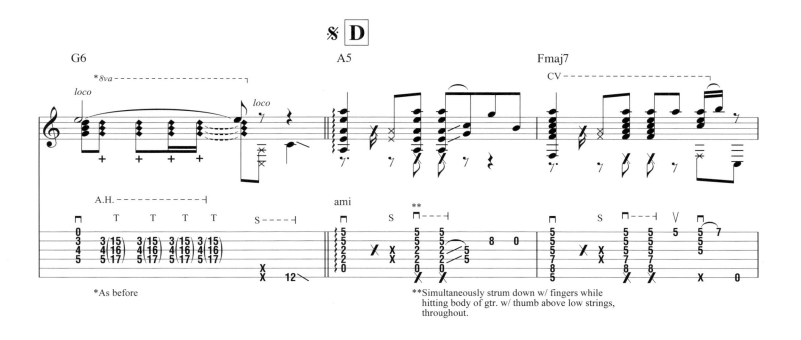

*As before

**Simultaneously strum down w/ fingers while hitting body of gtr. w/ thumb above low strings, throughout.

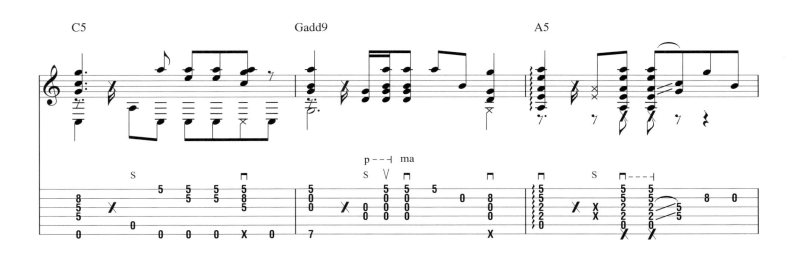

To Coda 2 ⊕

To Coda 1 ⊕

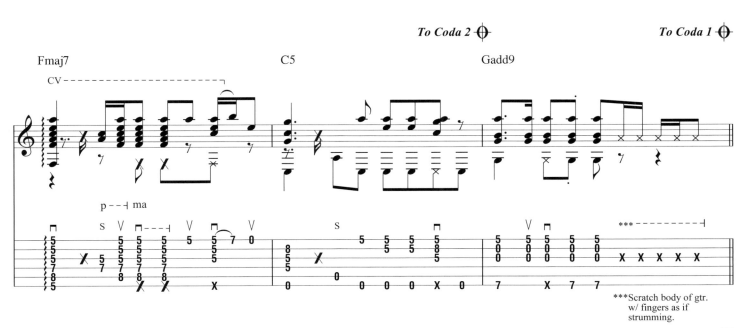

***Scratch body of gtr. w/ fingers as if strumming.

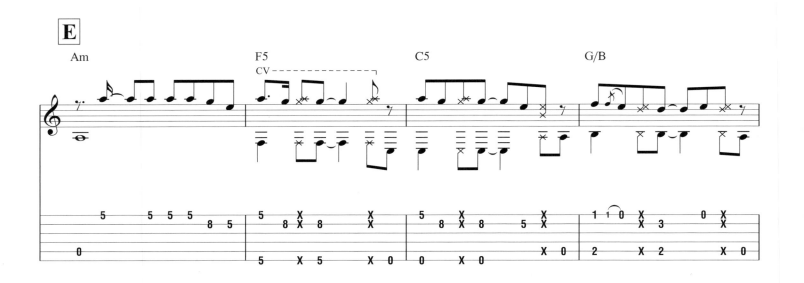

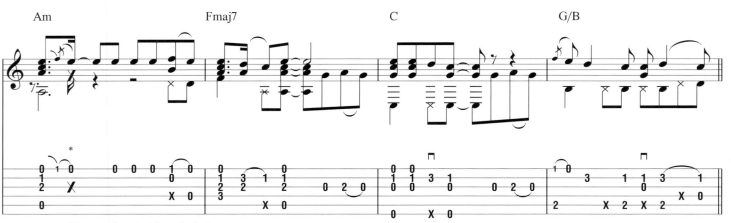

*Tap soundboard w/ finger (golpe).

F

Fmaj7   G6

Whispered: Caught in the un - der - tow, ___ just caught in the un - der - tow. ___

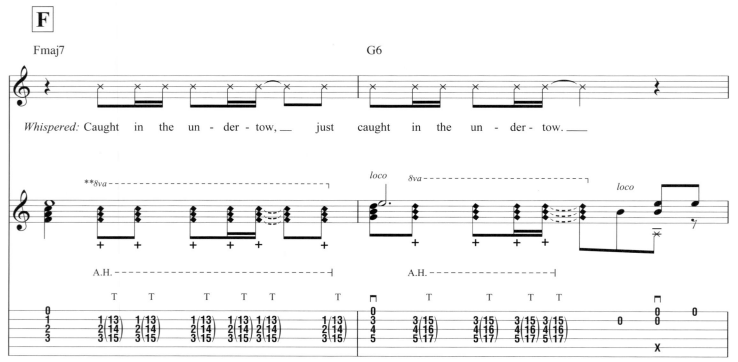

**Refers to downstemmed notes only, next 2 meas.

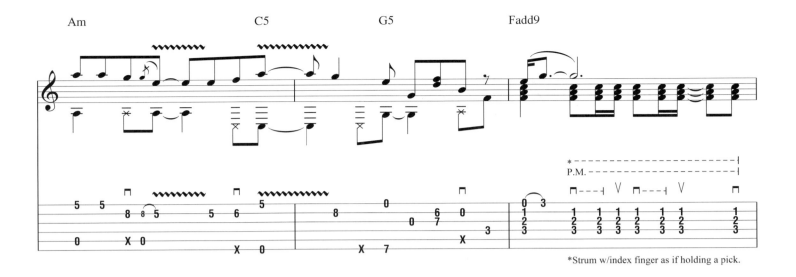

*Strum w/index finger as if holding a pick.

D.S. al Coda 1

**As before

⊕ **Coda 1**

G

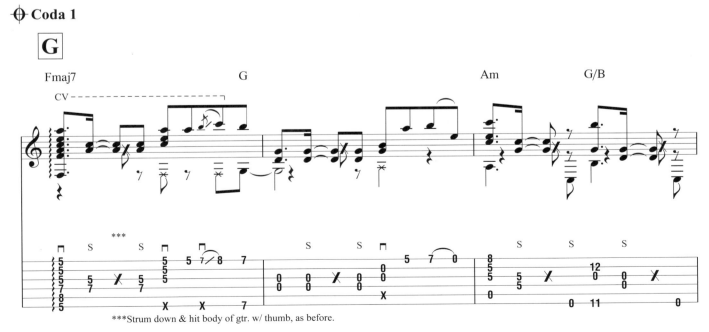

***Strum down & hit body of gtr. w/ thumb, as before.

D.S. al Coda 2

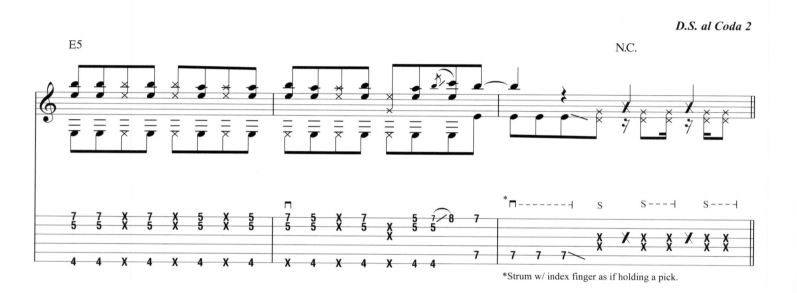

*Strum w/ index finger as if holding a pick.

⊕ **Coda 2**

H

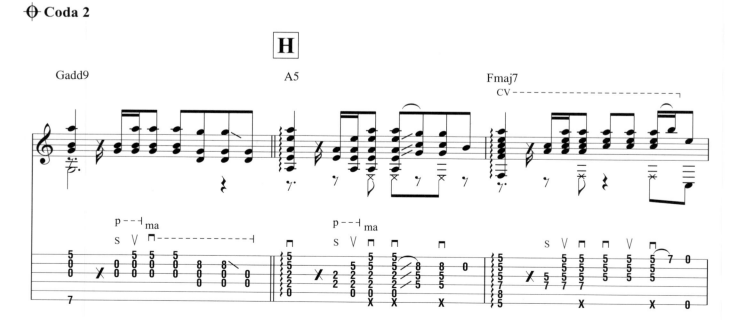

I'm tired of be-ing what you want _____ me to be. _____

I'm tired of be-ing what you want _____ me to be. _____

Smells Like Teen Spirit

Words and Music by Kurt Cobain, Krist Novoselic and Dave Grohl

Tune down 1 step:
(low to high) D-G-C-F-A-D

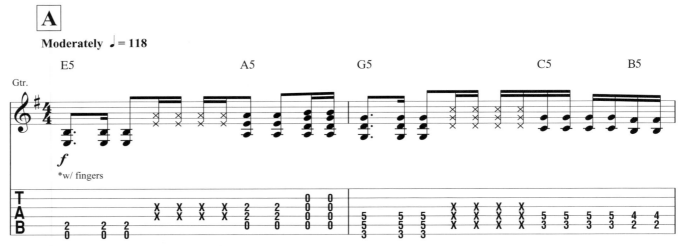

*Strum w/ index finger as if holding a pick, next 3 meas.

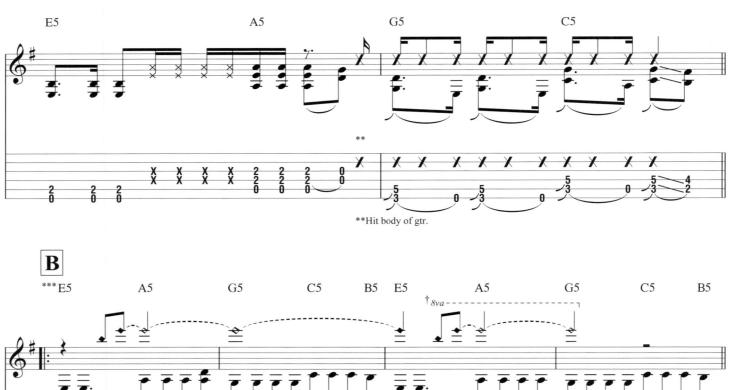

**Hit body of gtr.

***Chord symbols reflect implied harmony.

Pitch: B   E

†Refers to upstemmed notes only.

Copyright © 1991 The End Of Music, Primary Wave Tunes, M.J. Twelve Music and Murky Slough Music
This arrangement Copyright © 2017 The End Of Music, Primary Wave Tunes, M.J. Twelve Music and Murky Slough Music
All Rights for The End Of Music and Primary Wave Tunes Administered by BMG Rights Management (US) LLC
All Rights Reserved   Used by Permission

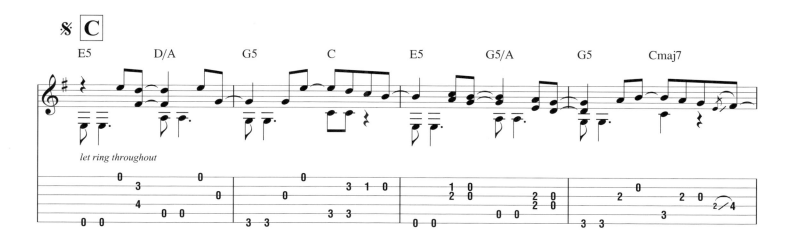

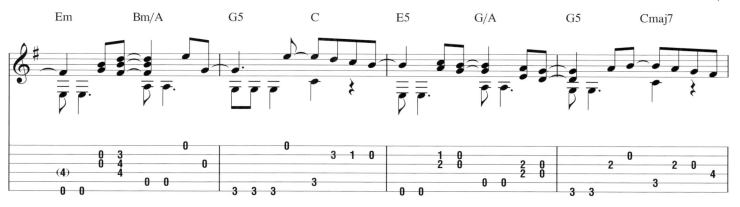

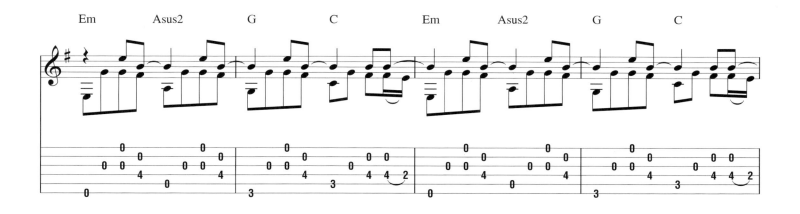

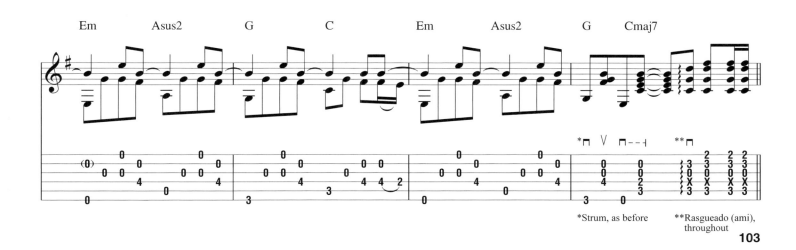

2nd & 3rd times, Gtr. 1: w/ Rhy. Fill 2

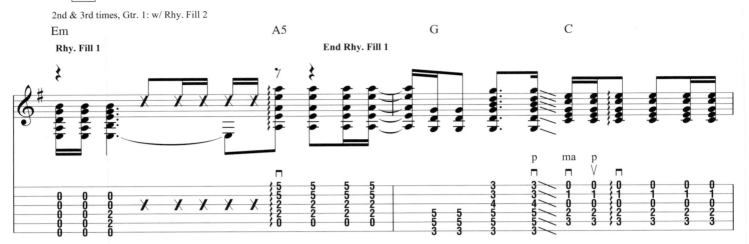

2nd & 3rd times, Gtr. 1: w/ Rhy. Fill 2

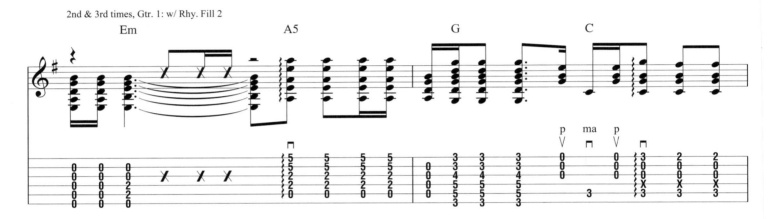

To Coda 2 ⊕

2nd & 3rd times, Gtr. 1: w/ Rhy. Fill 2

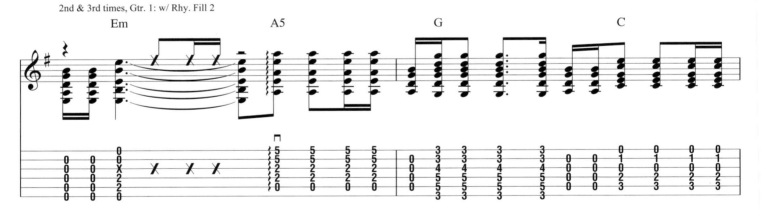

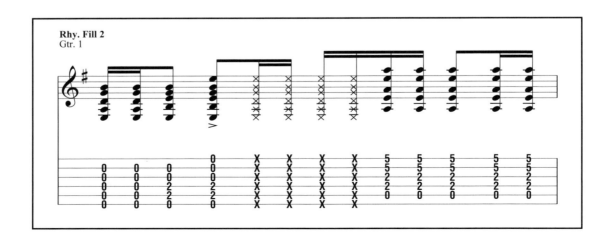

2nd & 3rd times, Gtr. 1: w/ Rhy. Fill 2

2nd time, Gtr. 1: w/ Rhy. Fill 1

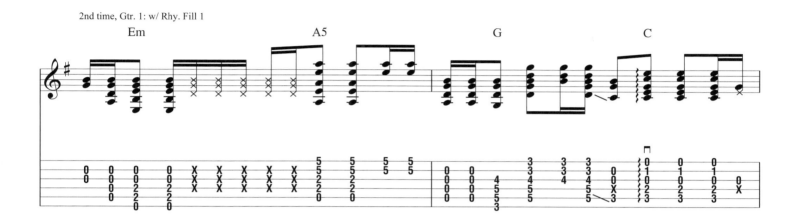

2nd time, Gtr. 1: w/ Rhy. Fill 1

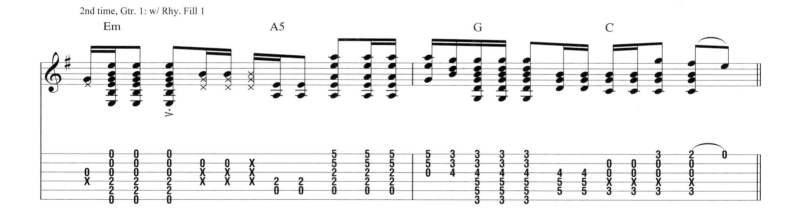

E

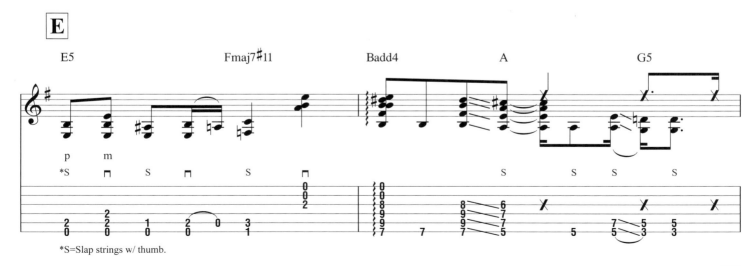

*S=Slap strings w/ thumb.

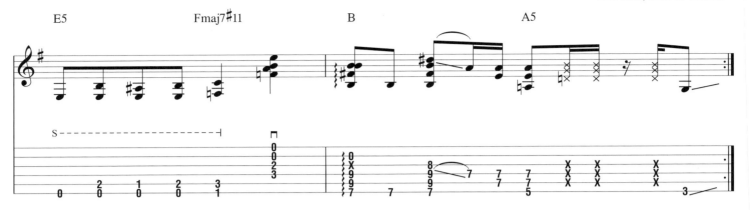

Coda 1

Lo, hel-lo, ___ hel lo, ___ hel lo, ___ how low? Hel lo, ___ hel-lo, ___ hel-lo, ___ how low? ___

___ Hel-lo, ___ hel - lo, ___ hel - lo, ___ how low? ___ Hel-lo, ___ hel - lo. ___

Coda 2

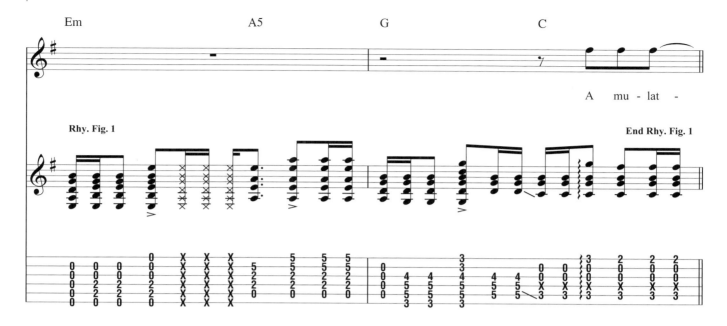

A mu - lat -

Rhy. Fig. 1 ...... **End Rhy. Fig. 1**

 G

Gtr. 1: w/ Rhy. Fig. 1 (6 times)

- to, an al - bi - no, a mos - qui - to, my li - bi - do. A de - ni -

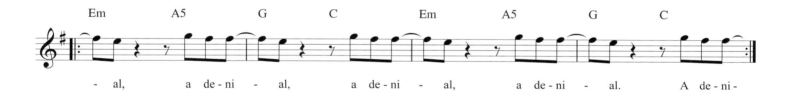

- al, a de - ni - al, a de - ni - al, a de - ni - al. A de - ni -

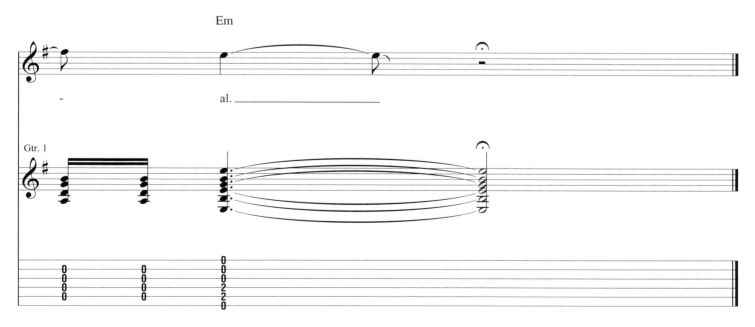

- al. _____

Gtr. 1

107

Stand by Me

Words and Music by Jerry Leiber, Mike Stoller and Ben E. King

Drop D tuning, down 1/2 step, capo II:
(low to high) D♭-A♭-D♭-G♭-B♭-E♭

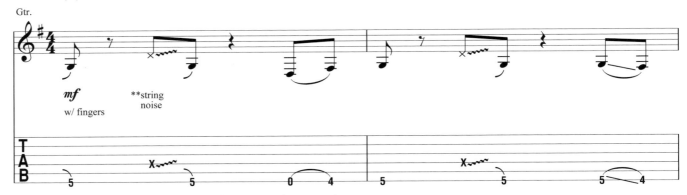

*Symbols in parentheses represent chord names respective to capoed gtr.
Capoed fret is "0" in tab. Chord symbols reflect implied harmony.

**String noise produced by sliding pick-hand
middle finger on string, next 8 meas.

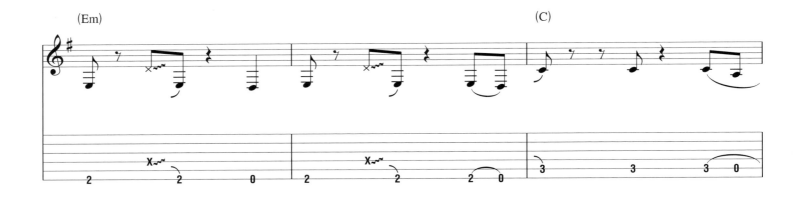

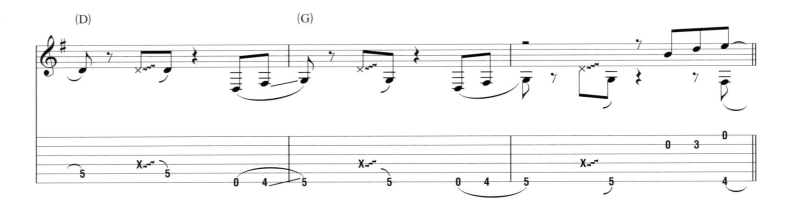

Copyright © 1961 Sony/ATV Music Publishing LLC
Copyright Renewed
This arrangement Copyright © 2017 Sony/ATV Music Publishing LLC
All Rights Administered by Sony/ATV Music Publishing LLC, 424 Church Street, Suite 1200, Nashville, TN 37219
International Copyright Secured   All Rights Reserved

2nd time, Gtr. 1: w/ Fill 1

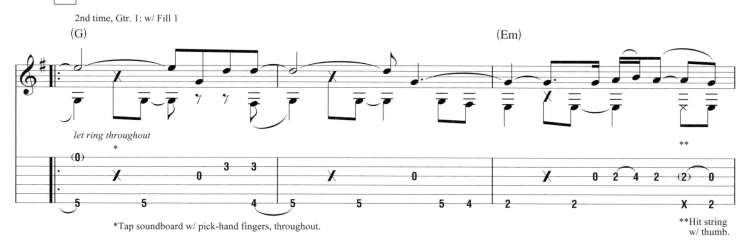

*Tap soundboard w/ pick-hand fingers, throughout.

**Hit string w/ thumb.

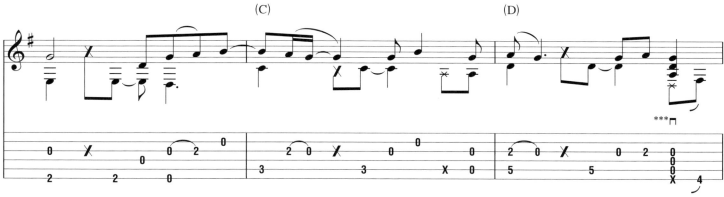

***In a single downstroke, sound upstemmed notes by striking strings w/ backs of fingernails while slapping thumb against strings to produce a percussive sound (downstemmed notes), throughout.

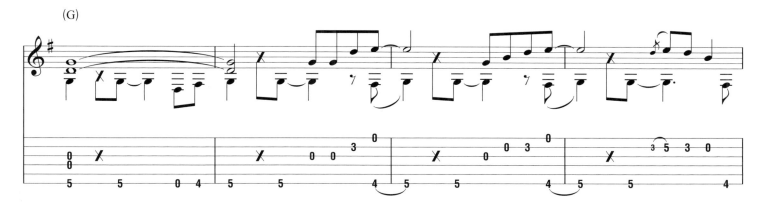

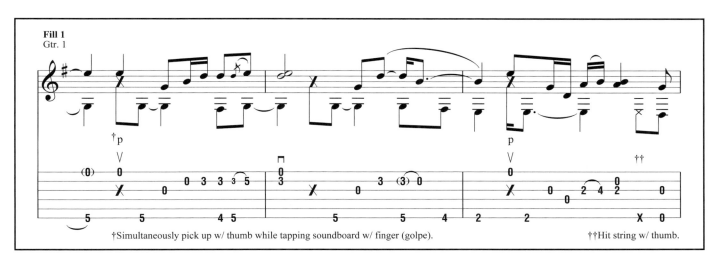

†Simultaneously pick up w/ thumb while tapping soundboard w/ finger (golpe).

††Hit string w/ thumb.

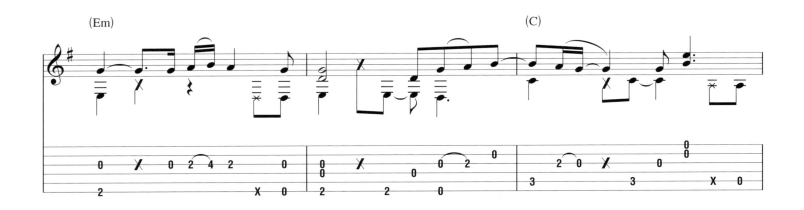

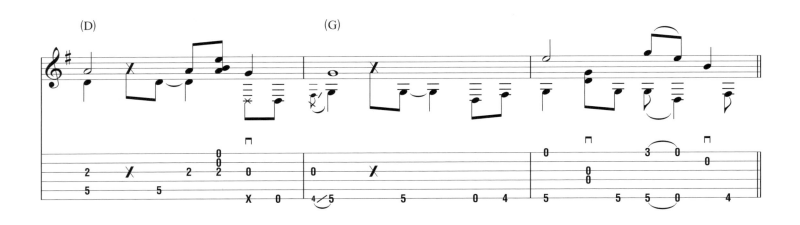

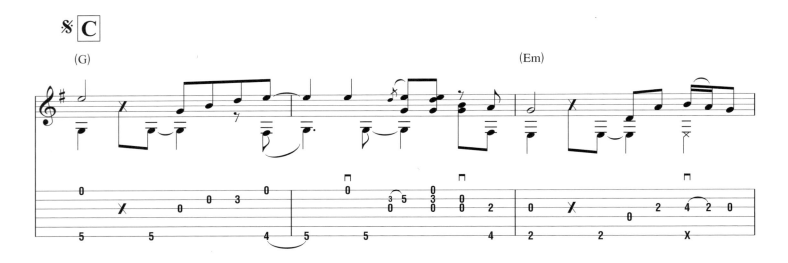

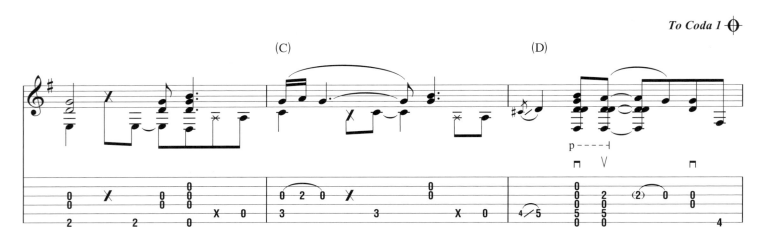

*Rasgueado (ami), throughout

D.S. al Coda 1

⊕ Coda 1

D.S. al Coda 2
(take 2nd ending)

⊕ Coda 2

E

*string noise

**String noise produced by sliding pick-hand
middle finger on string, till end.*

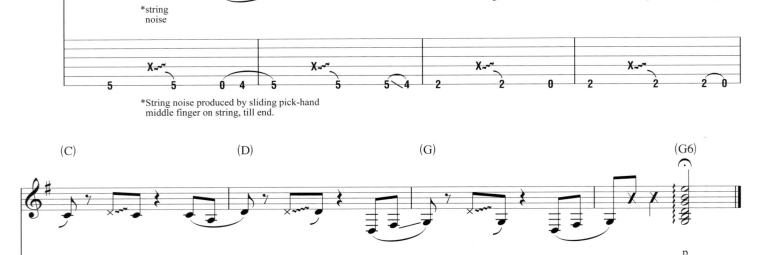

Still Got the Blues

Words and Music by Gary Moore

Tune down 1 step:
(low to high) D-G-C-F-A-D

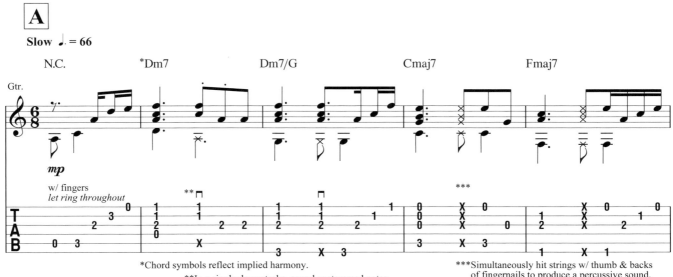

*Chord symbols reflect implied harmony.

**In a single downstroke, sound upstemmed notes
by striking strings w/ backs of fingernails while
slapping thumb against strings to produce a
percussive sound (downstemmed notes),
throughout.

***Simultaneously hit strings w/ thumb & backs
of fingernails to produce a percussive sound,
throughout.

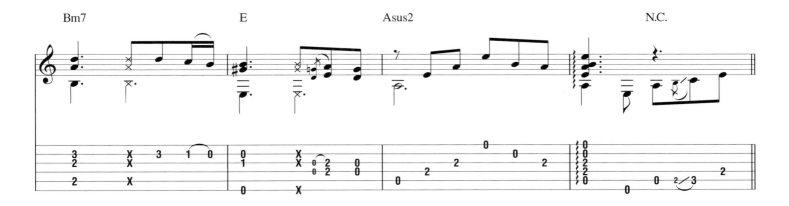

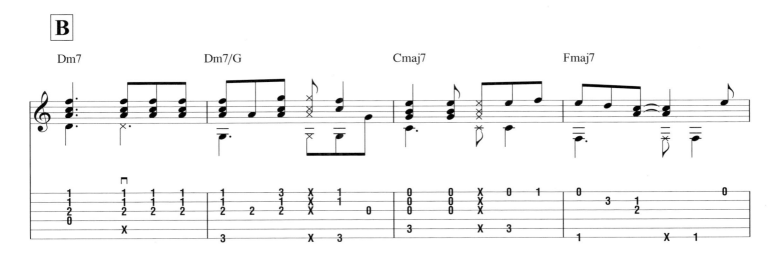

Copyright © 1990 Bonuswise Ltd.
This arrangement Copyright © 2017 Bonuswise Ltd.
All Rights Administered by BMG Rights Management (US) LLC
All Rights Reserved   Used by Permission

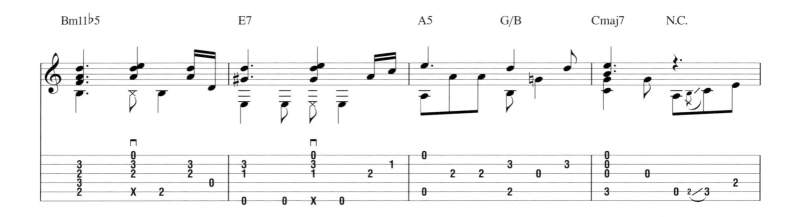

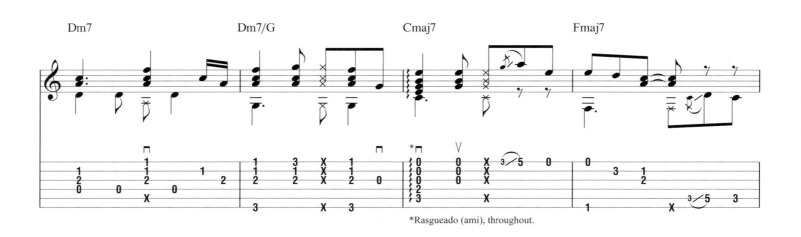

*Rasgueado (ami), throughout.

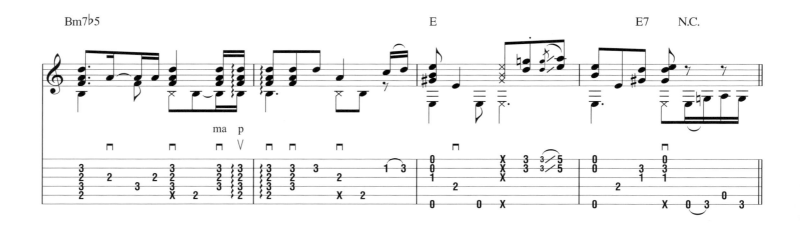

C

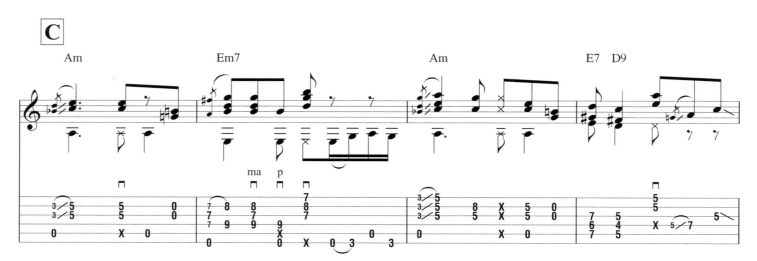

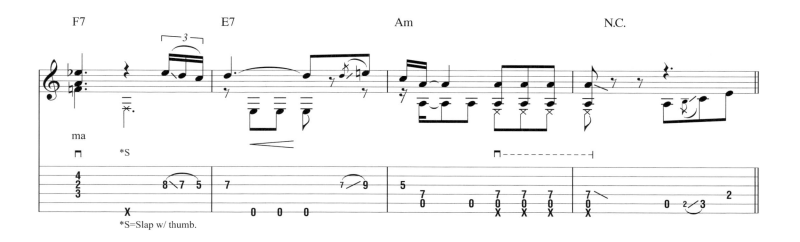

*S=Slap w/ thumb.

D

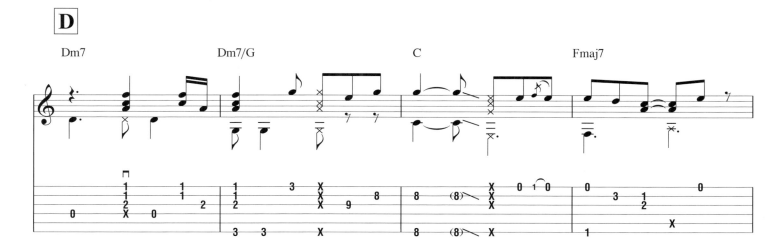

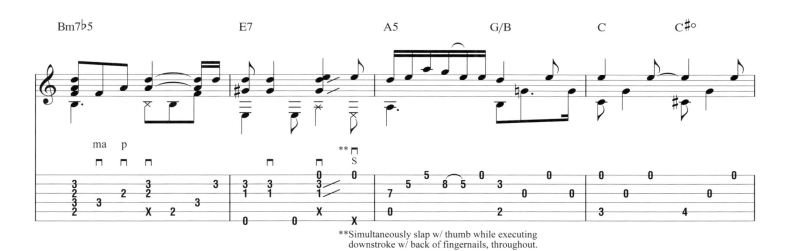

**Simultaneously slap w/ thumb while executing
downstroke w/ back of fingernails, throughout.

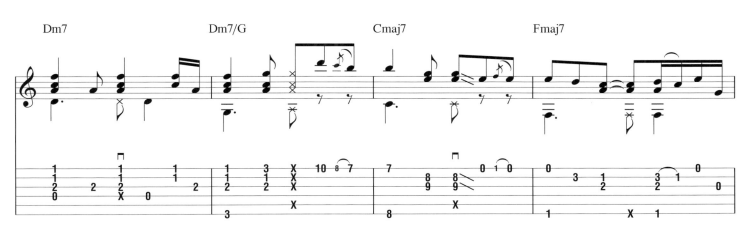

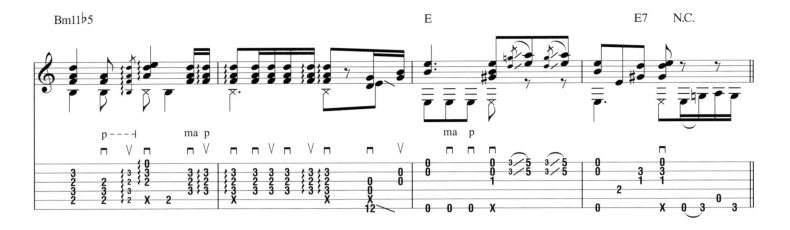

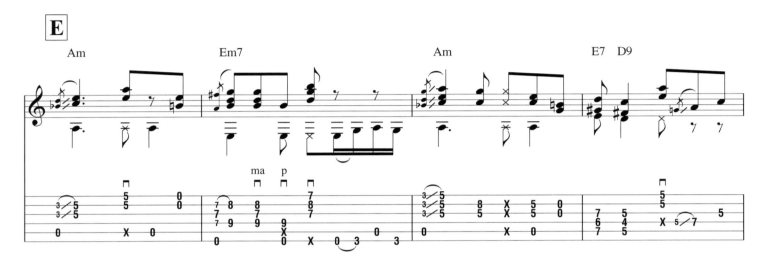

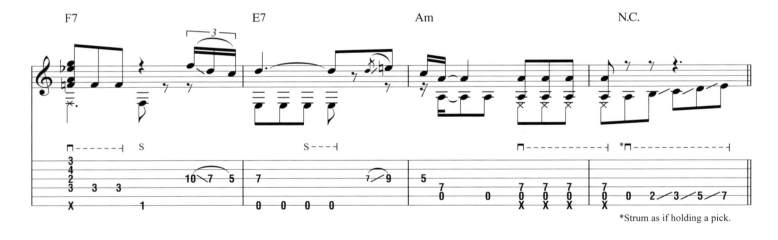

*Strum as if holding a pick.

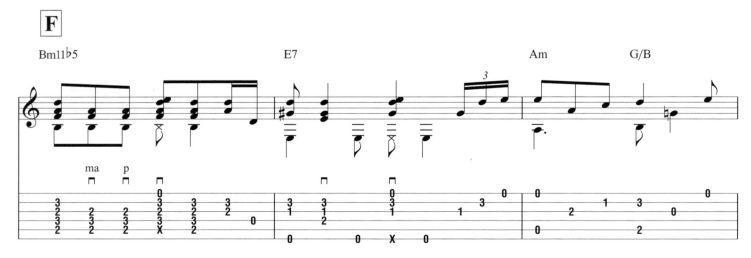

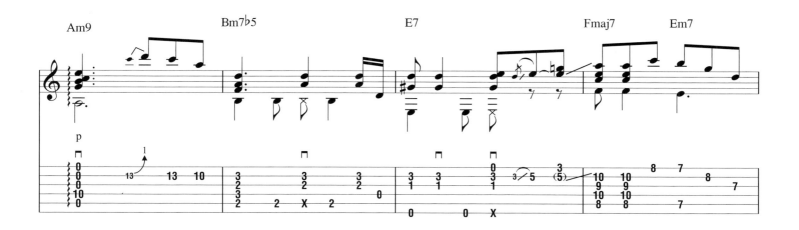

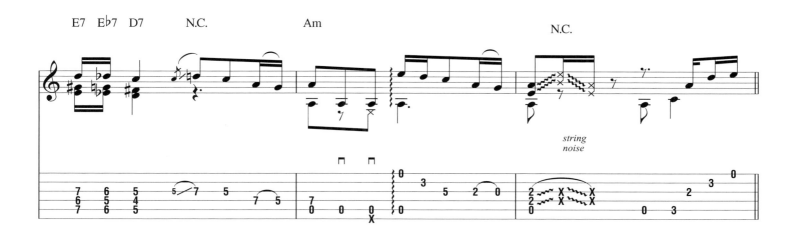

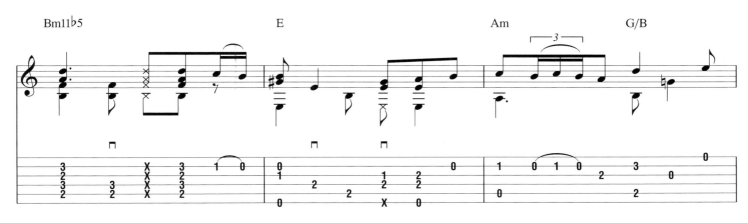

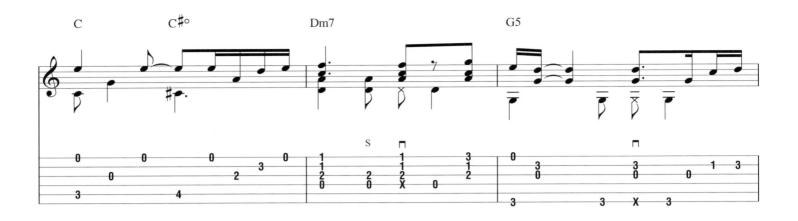

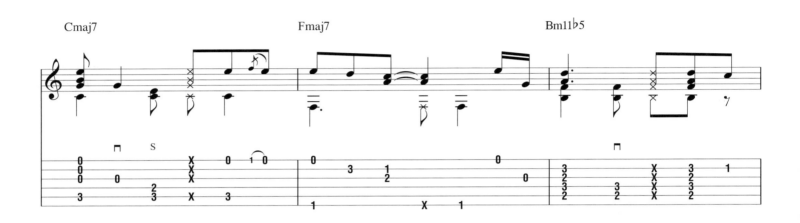

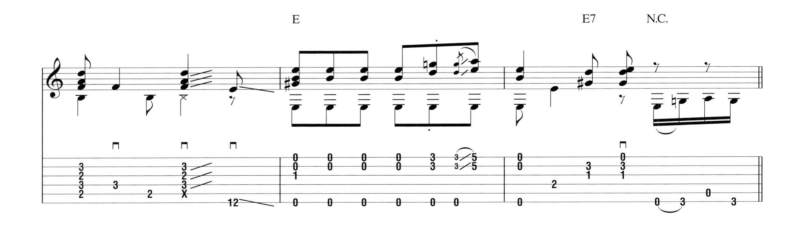

H

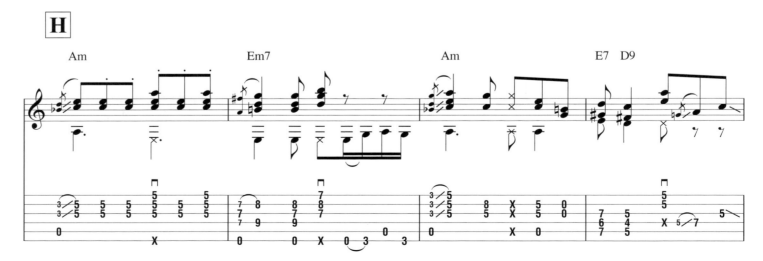

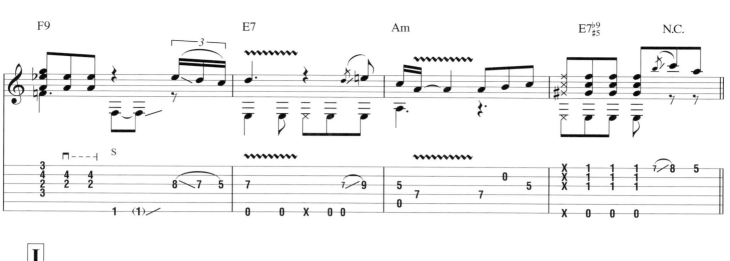

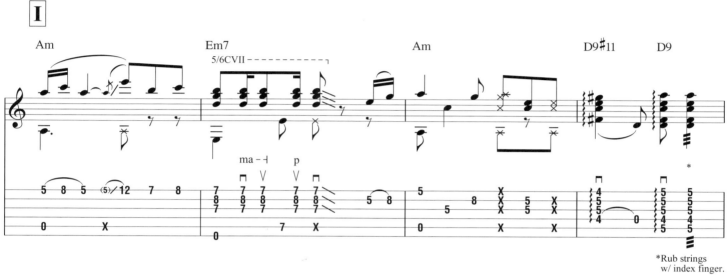

*Rub strings
w/ index finger.

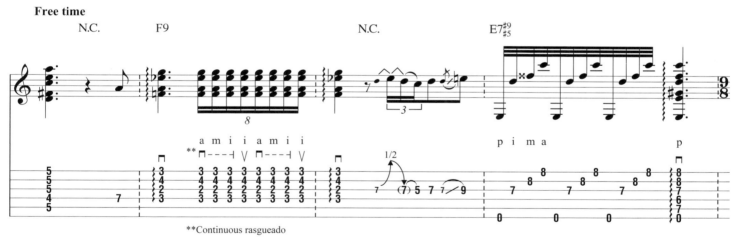

**Continuous rasgueado

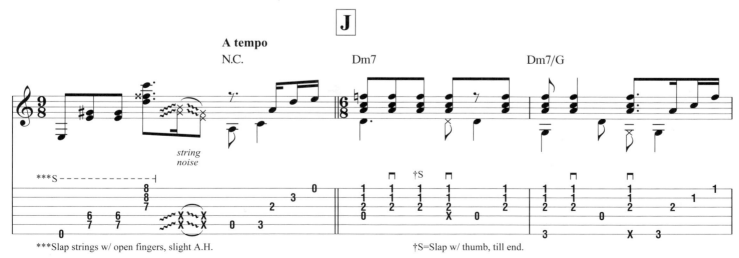

***Slap strings w/ open fingers, slight A.H.   †S=Slap w/ thumb, till end.

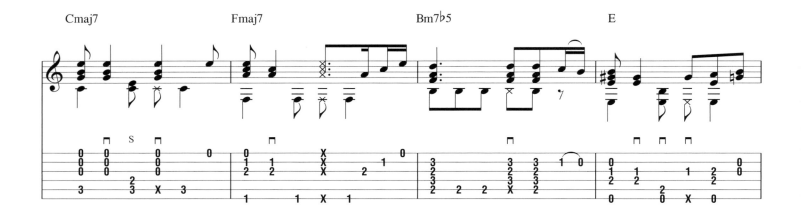

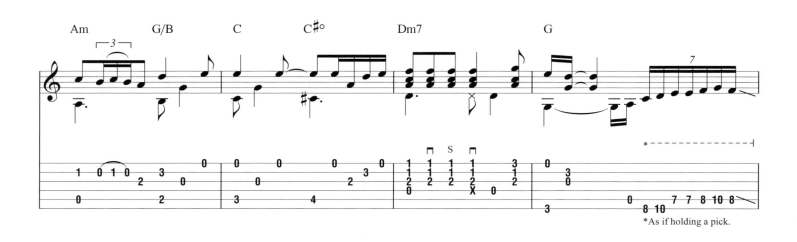

*As if holding a pick.

Free time

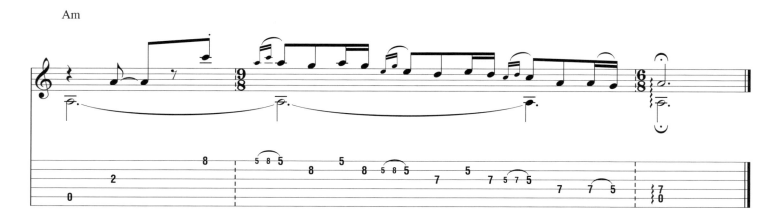

Still Loving You

Words and Music by Rudolf Schenker and Klaus Meine

Tune down 1/2 step, capo II:
(low to high) Eb-Ab-Db-Gb-Bb-Eb

Moderately ♩ = 106

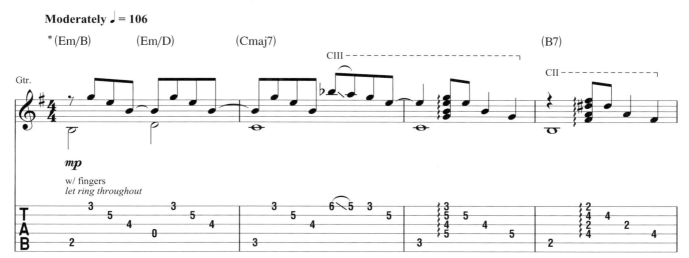

*Symbols in parentheses represent chord names respective to capoed guitar.
 Capoed fret is "0" in tab.
 Chord symbols reflect implied harmony.

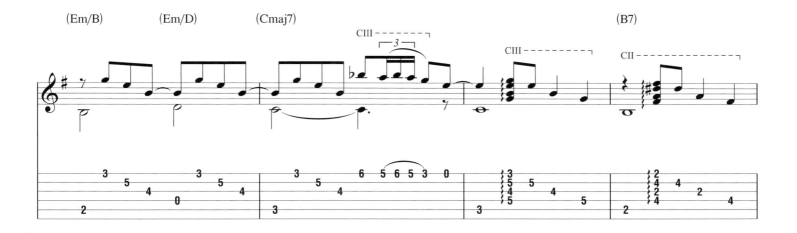

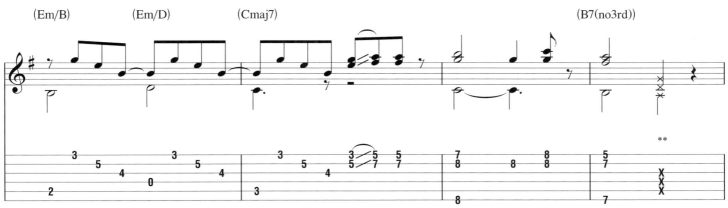

**Simultaneously hit strings w/ thumb
& backs of fingernails to produce a
percussive sound, throughout.

Copyright © 1984 by Edition Arabella Music Muenchen
This arrangement Copyright © 2017 by Edition Arabella Music Muenchen
All Rights for the U.S. Administered by Universal Music - MGB Songs
International Copyright Secured   All Rights Reserved

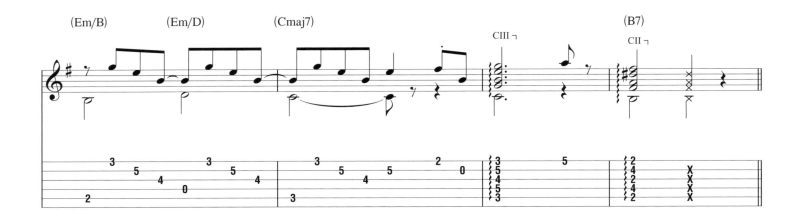

B

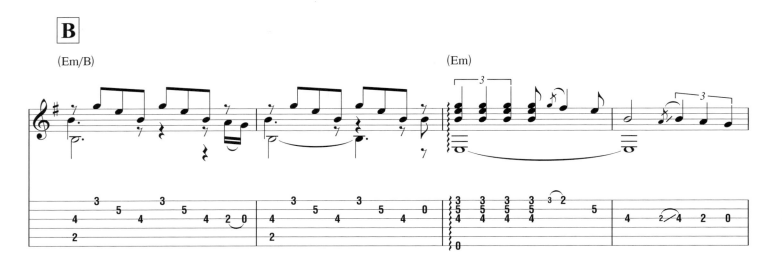

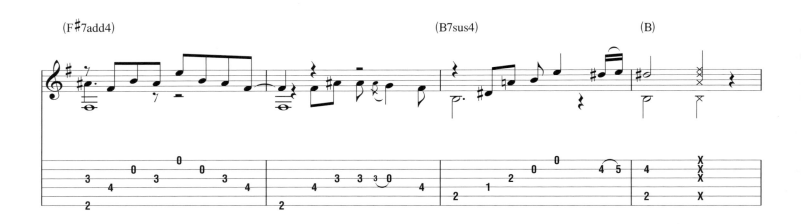

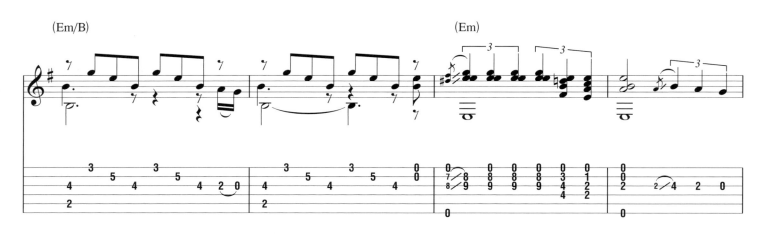

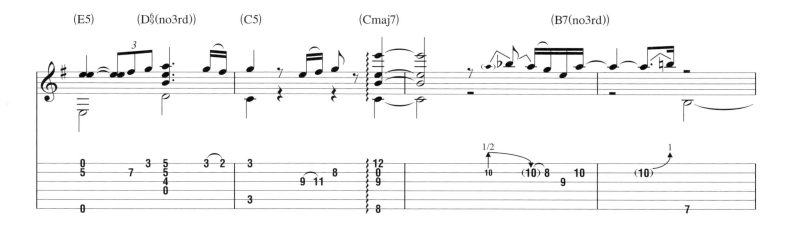

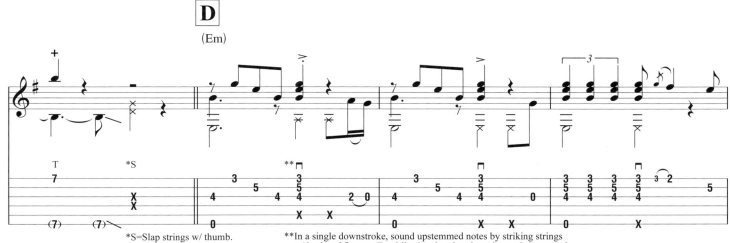

*S=Slap strings w/ thumb.

**In a single downstroke, sound upstemmed notes by striking strings
w/ backs of fingernails while slapping thumb against strings to produce
a percussive sound (downstemmed notes), throughout.

*Artificial harmonics produced by tapping
strings at frets indicated in parentheses.

**Hit string w/ index finger.

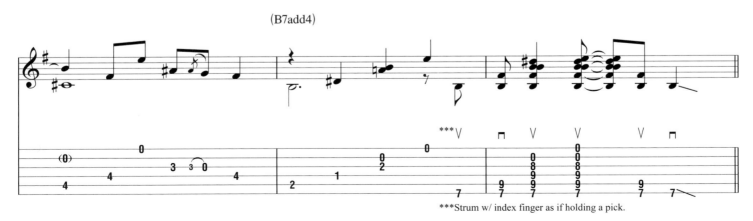

***Strum w/ index finger as if holding a pick.

E

*Rasgueado (ami), throughout.
**w/ backs of fingernails

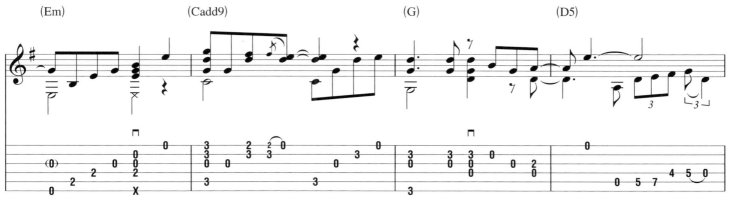

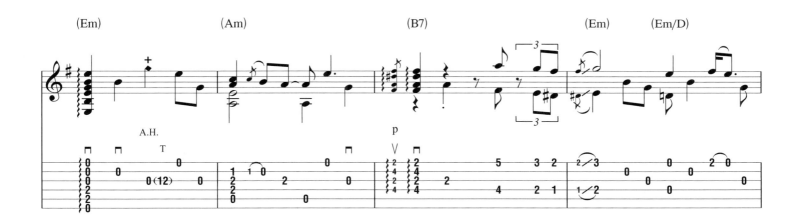

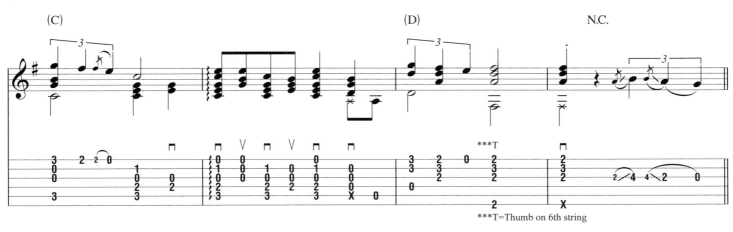

***T=Thumb on 6th string

F

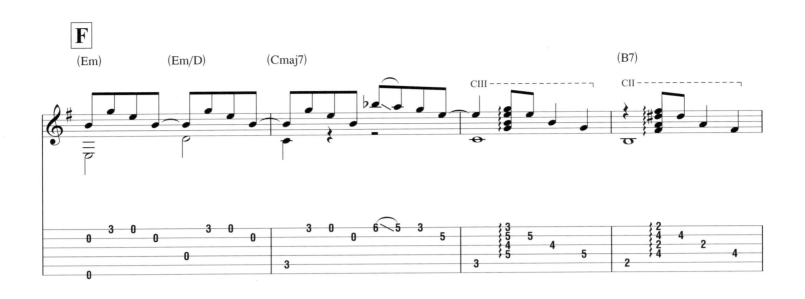

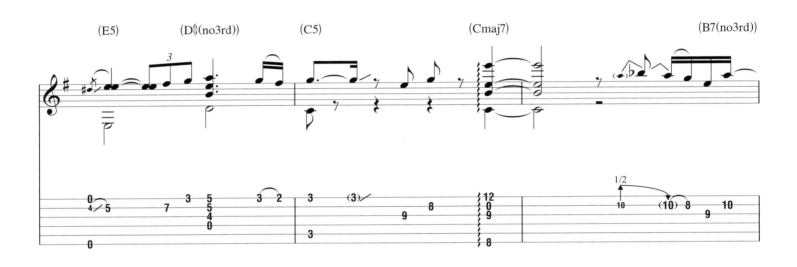

G

*Slap w/ open fingers of pick hand.

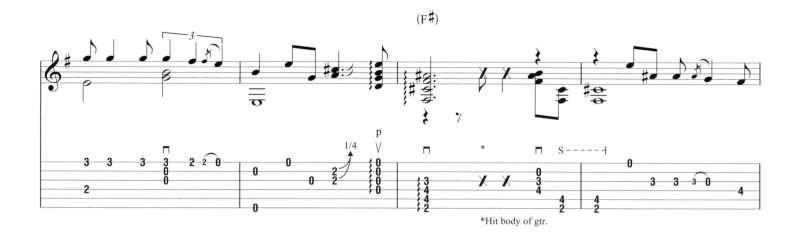

(F#)

*Hit body of gtr.

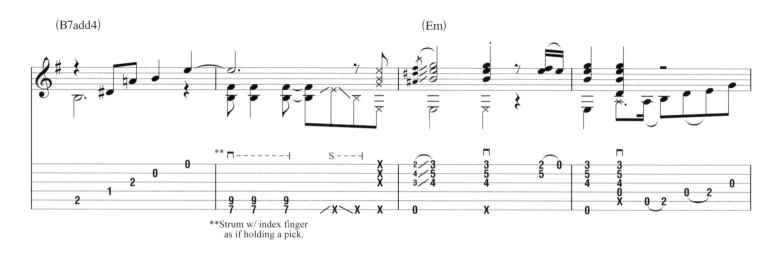

(B7add4)   (Em)

**Strum w/ index finger
as if holding a pick.

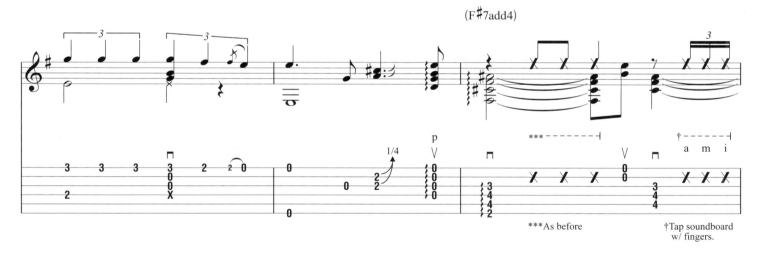

(F#7add4)

***As before   †Tap soundboard
                                    w/ fingers.

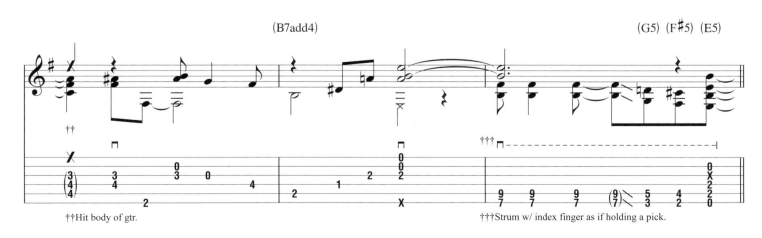

(B7add4)   (G5) (F#5) (E5)

††Hit body of gtr.   †††Strum w/ index finger as if holding a pick.

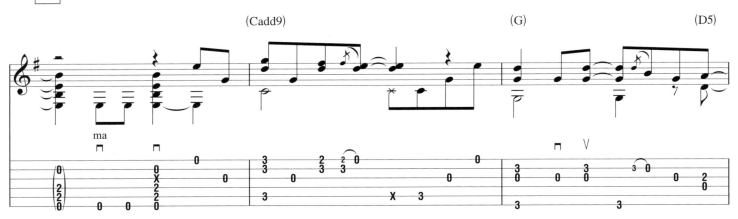

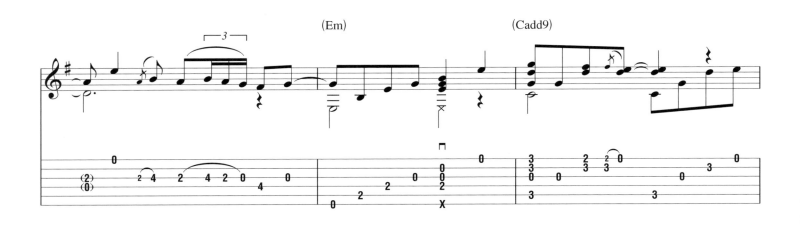

*Strum w/ index finger
as if holding a pick.

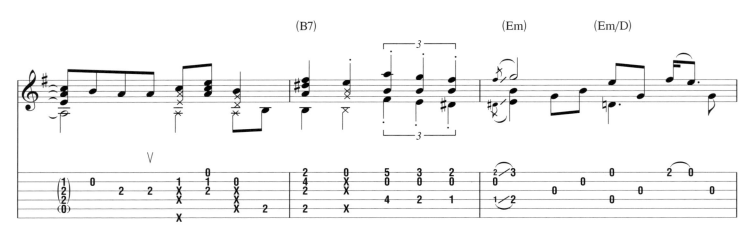

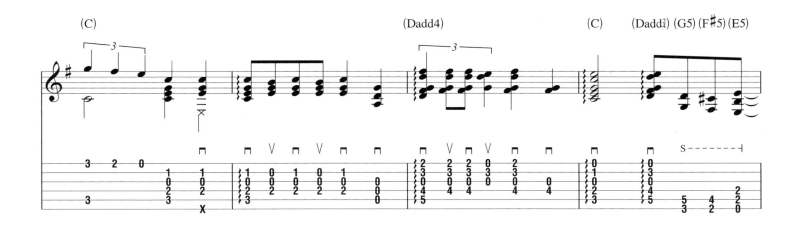

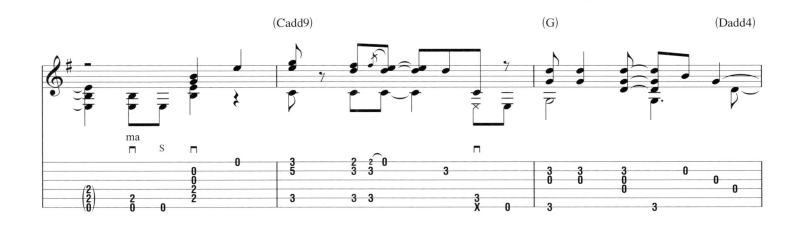

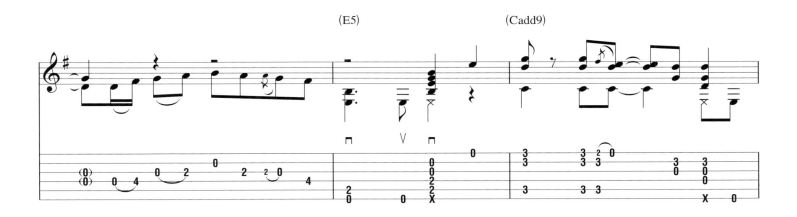

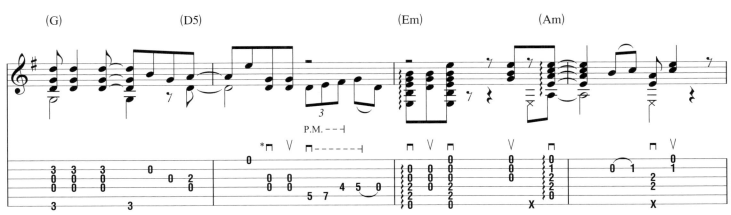

*Strum w/ index finger as if holding a pick.

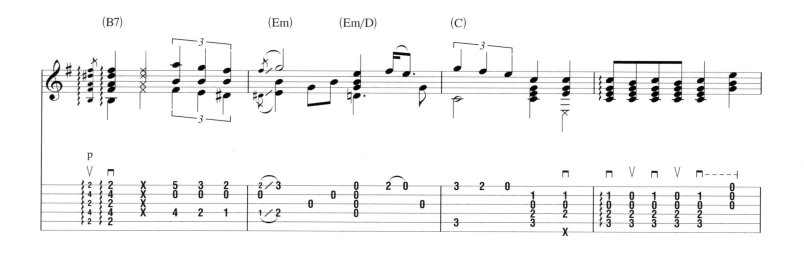

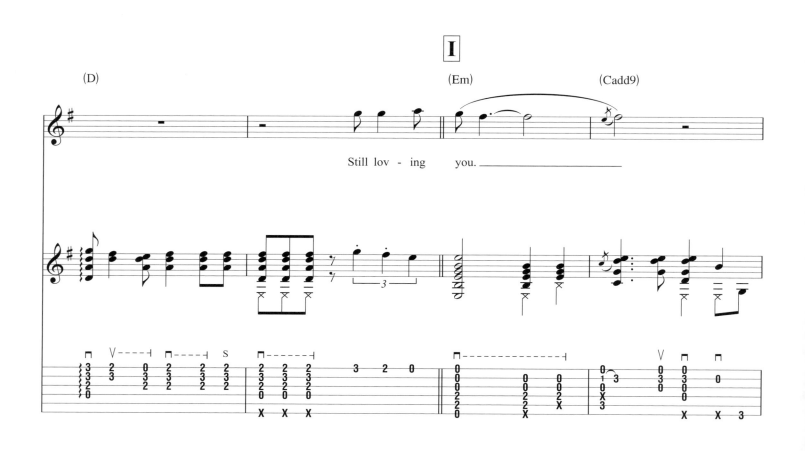

Still lov - ing you. _____

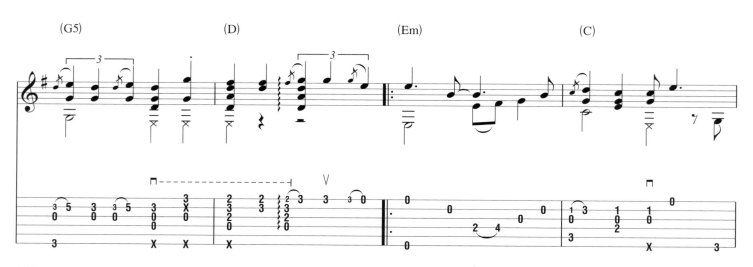

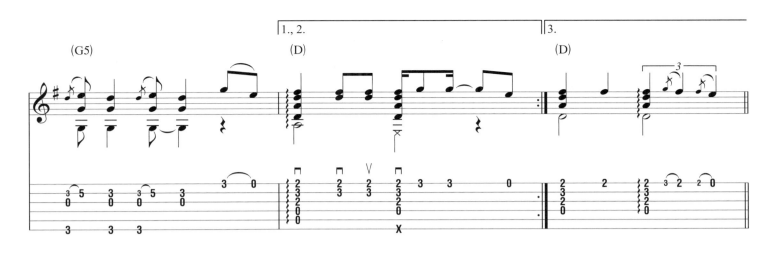

J

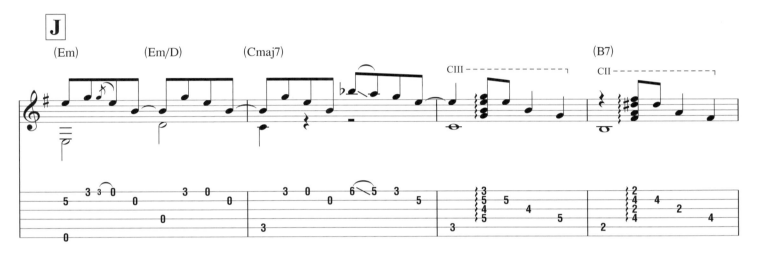

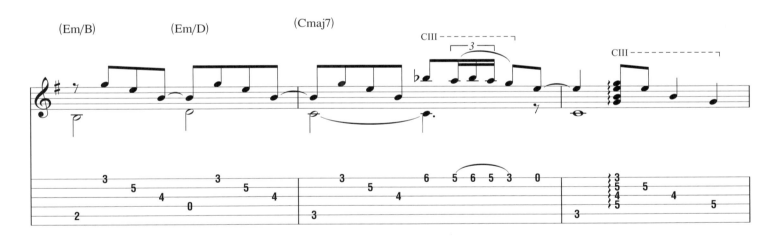

Free time

Sweet Child o' Mine

Words and Music by W. Axl Rose, Slash, Izzy Stradlin', Duff McKagan and Steven Adler

Tune down 1 step:
(low to high) D-G-C-F-A-D

Moderately fast ♩ = 132

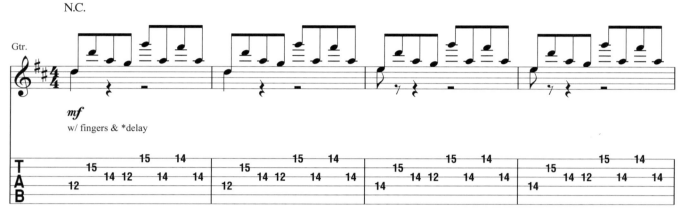

*Set for dotted eighth-note regeneration w/ 1 repeat.

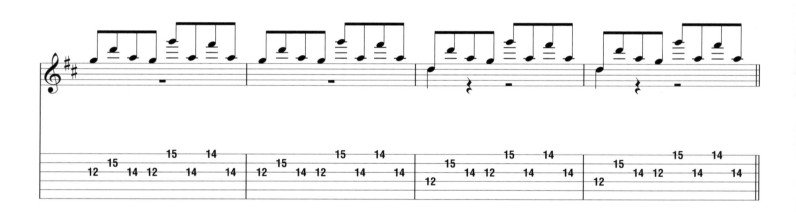

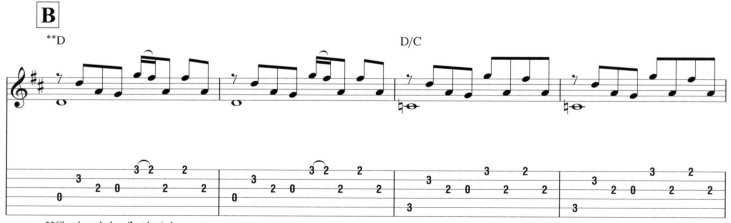

**Chord symbols reflect basic harmony.

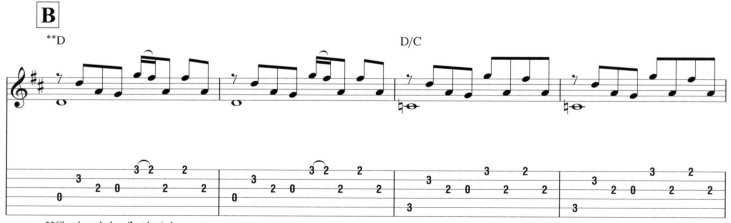

Copyright © 1987 Guns N' Roses Music (ASCAP) and Black Frog Music (ASCAP)
This arrangement Copyright © 2017 Guns N' Roses Music (ASCAP) and Black Frog Music (ASCAP)
All Rights for Black Frog Music in the U.S. and Canada Controlled and Administered by Universal - PolyGram International Publishing, Inc.
International Copyright Secured   All Rights Reserved

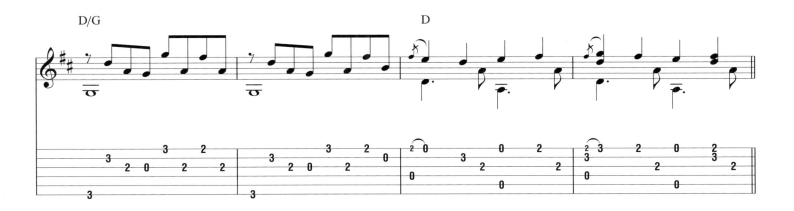

C

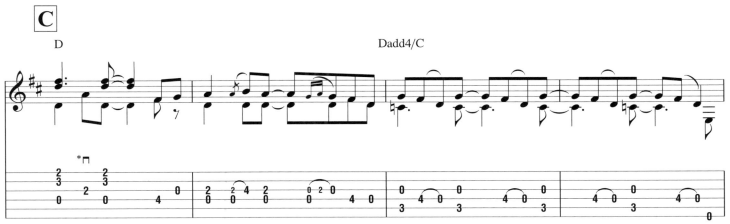

*Downstroke w/ back of fingernail.

**Strum w/ index finger
as if holding a pick.

D

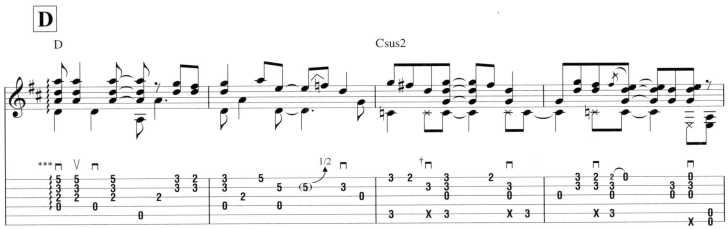

***Rasgueado (ami), throughout.

†In a single downstroke, sound upstemmed notes
by striking strings w/ backs of fingernails while
slapping thumb against strings to produce a percussive
sound (downstemmed notes), throughout.

*Simultaneously hit strings w/ thumb & backs of
fingernails to produce a percussive sound, throughout.

**Simultaneously tap soundboard
w/ fingers while strumming down
w/ thumb (golpe).

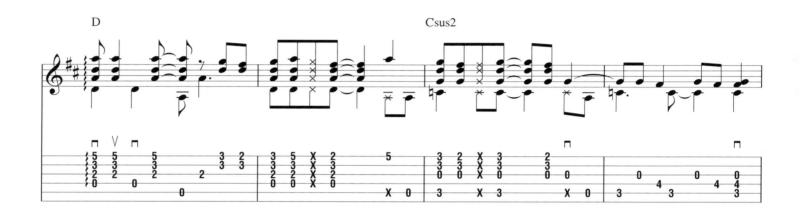

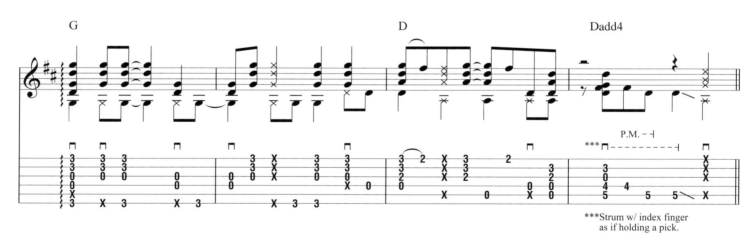

***Strum w/ index finger
as if holding a pick.

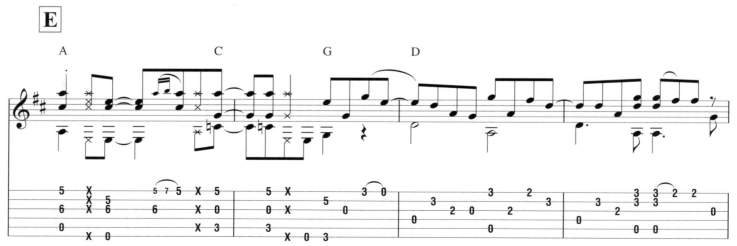

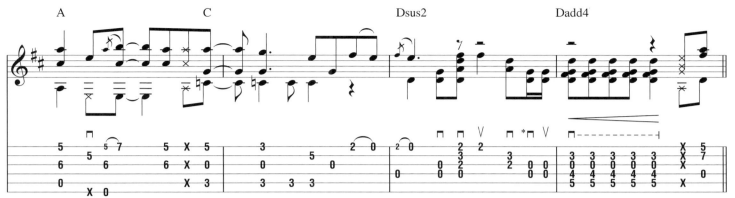

*Strum w/ index finger as if holding a pick.

F

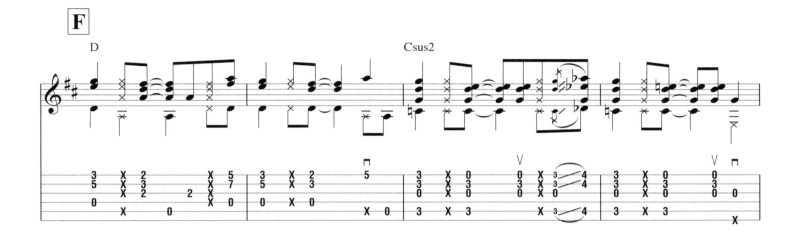

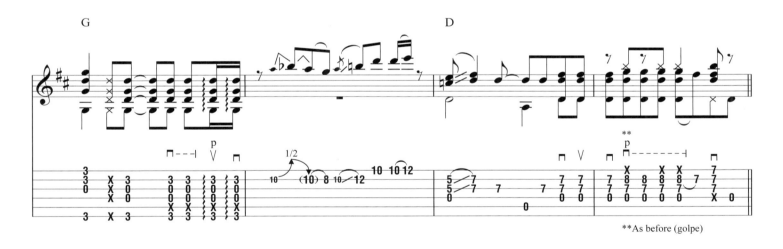

**As before (golpe)

G

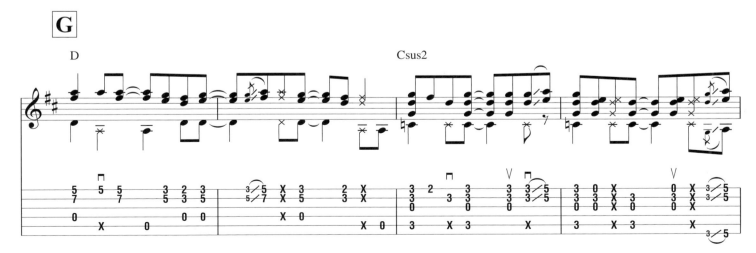

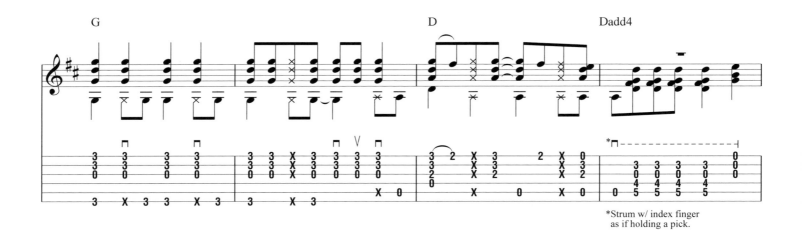

*Strum w/ index finger
as if holding a pick.

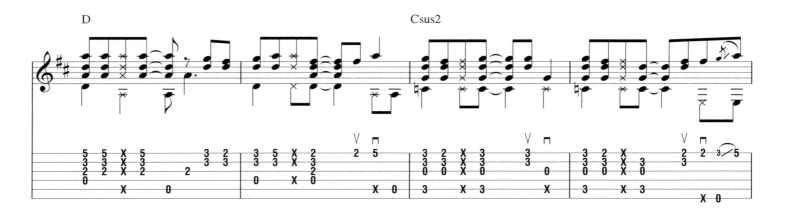

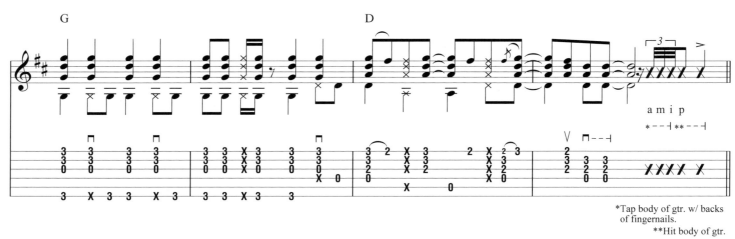

*Tap body of gtr. w/ backs
of fingernails.
**Hit body of gtr.

H

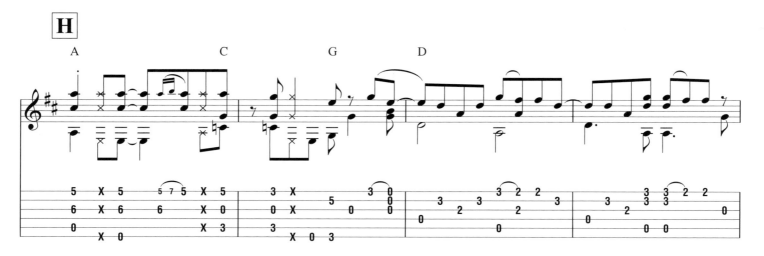

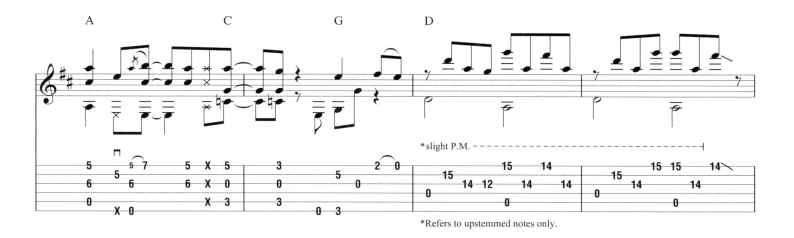

*slight P.M.

*Refers to upstemmed notes only.

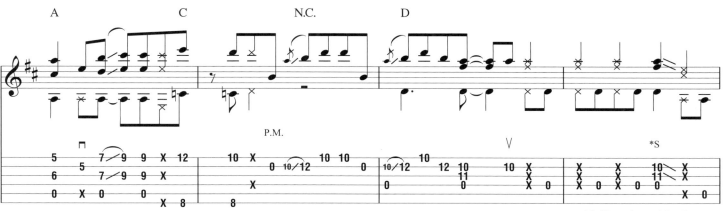

P.M.

*S=Slap strings w/ thumb,
refers to upstemmed notes only.

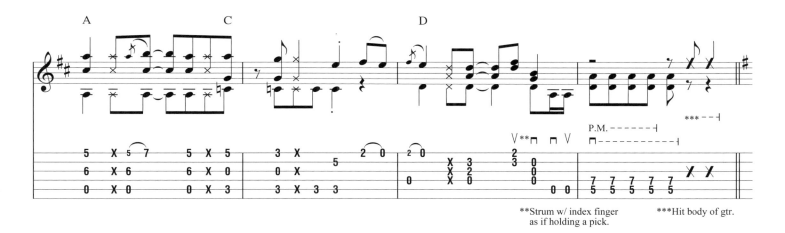

**Strum w/ index finger   ***Hit body of gtr.
as if holding a pick.

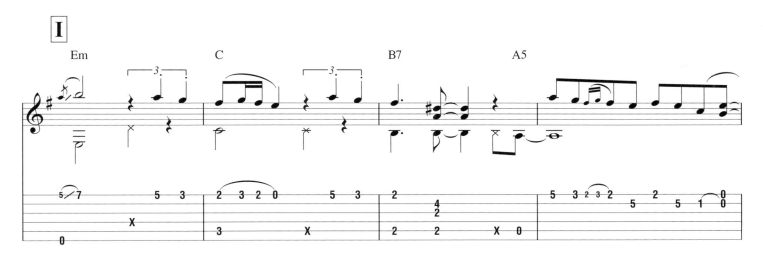

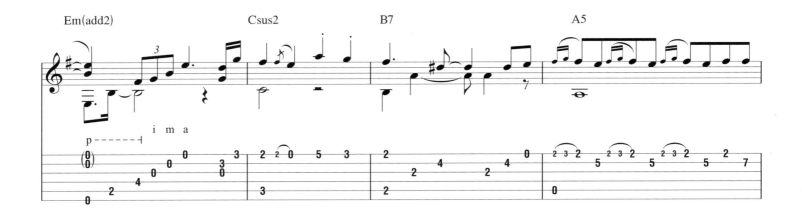

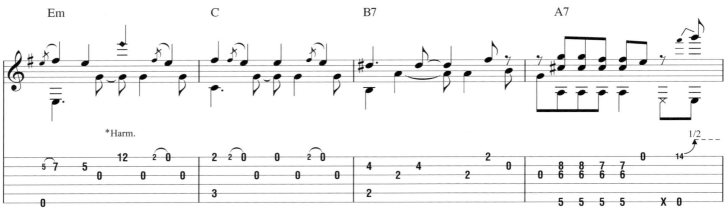

*Refers to upstemmed note only.

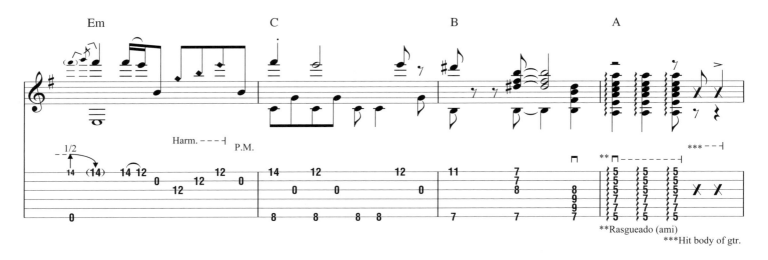

**Rasgueado (ami)
***Hit body of gtr.

J

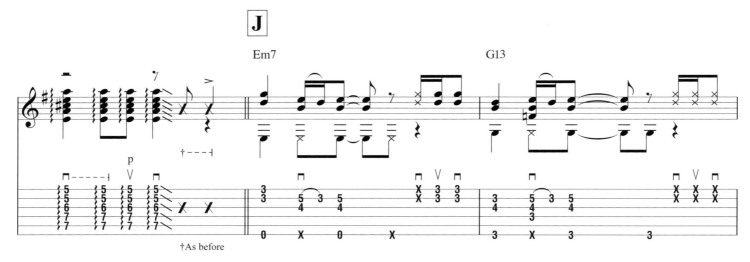

†As before

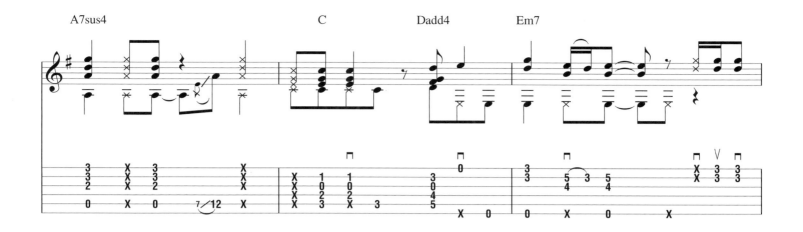

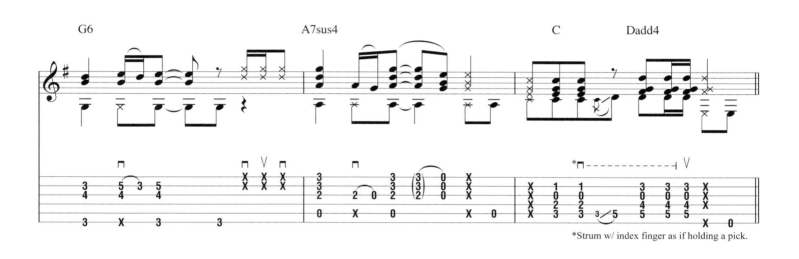

*Strum w/ index finger as if holding a pick.

K

Where do we go ____ now?   Where do we go ____ now?

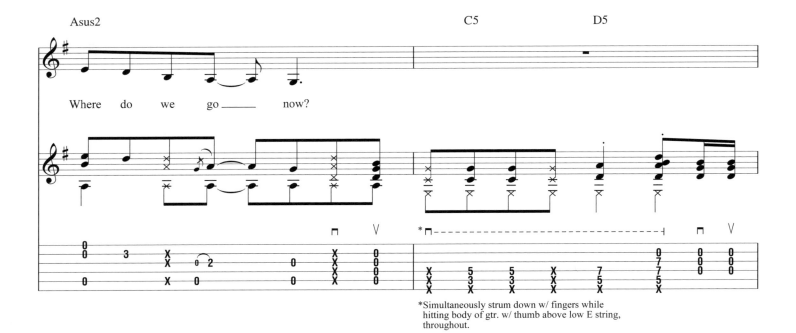

Where do we go ____ now?

*Simultaneously strum down w/ fingers while
hitting body of gtr. w/ thumb above low E string,
throughout.

Where do we go ____ now?   Where do we go ____ now?

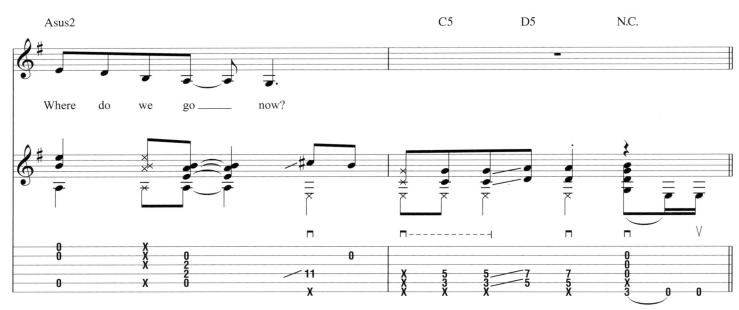

Where do we go ____ now?

L

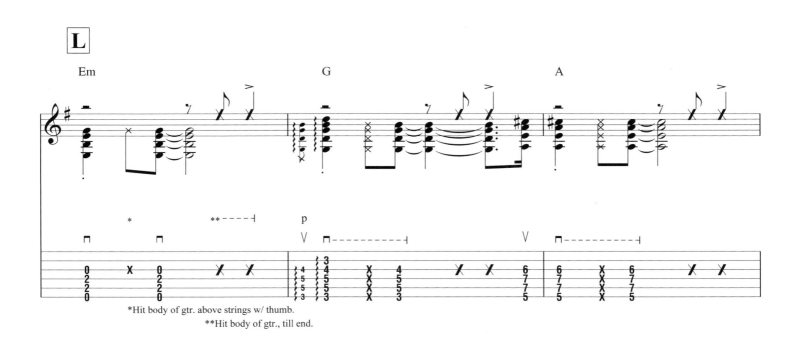

*Hit body of gtr. above strings w/ thumb.

**Hit body of gtr., till end.

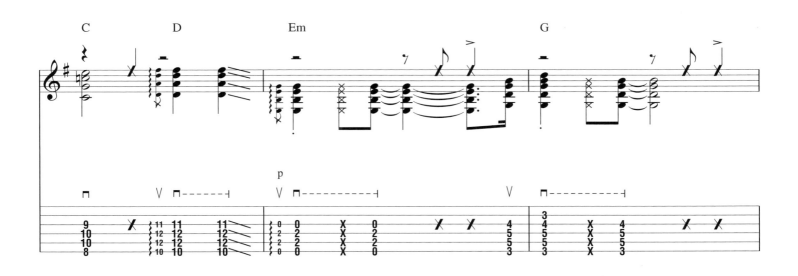

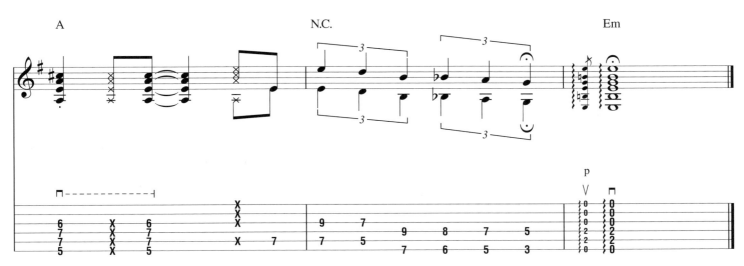

Zombie

Lyrics and Music by Dolores O'Riordan

Tune down 1/2 step:
(low to high) E♭-A♭-D♭-G♭-B♭-E♭

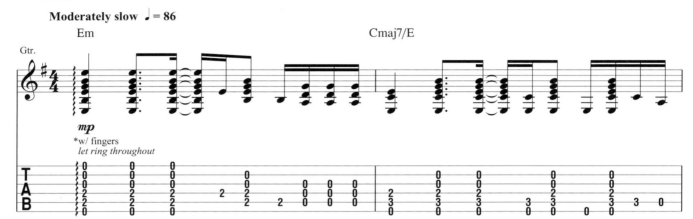

*w/ fingers
let ring throughout

*Strum w/ thumb & index finger as if holding a pick, next 12 meas.

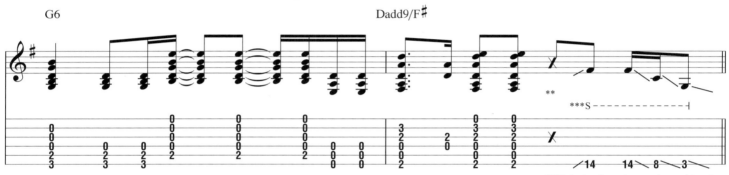

**Hit body of gtr. above strings w/ thumb.
***S=Slap strings w/ thumb, throughout.

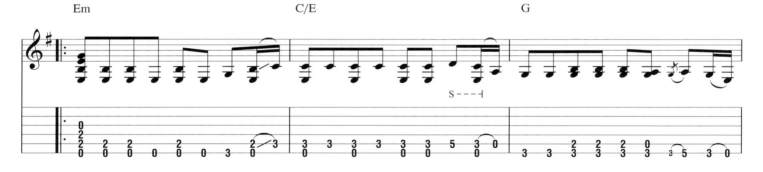

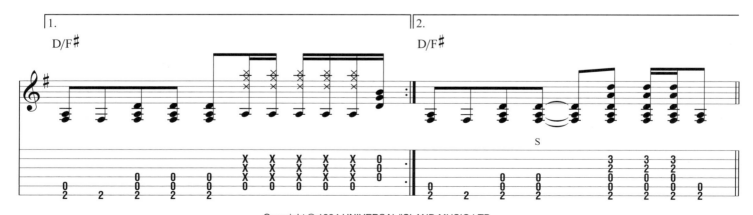

Copyright © 1994 UNIVERSAL/ISLAND MUSIC LTD.
This arrangement Copyright © 2017 UNIVERSAL/ISLAND MUSIC LTD.
All Rights for the U.S. and Canada Administered by UNIVERSAL - SONGS OF POLYGRAM INTERNATIONAL, INC.
All Rights Reserved   Used by Permission

*Rasgueado (ami), throughout.

**Harm.

**Refers to upstemmed notes only.

Harm.

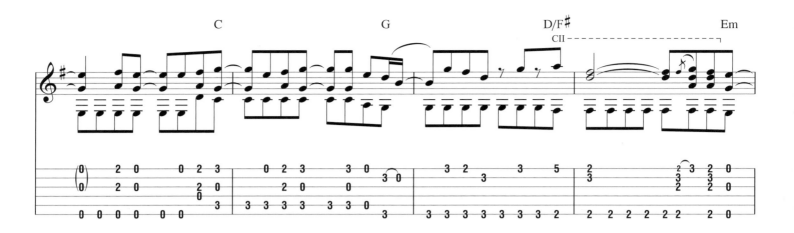

To Coda ⊕

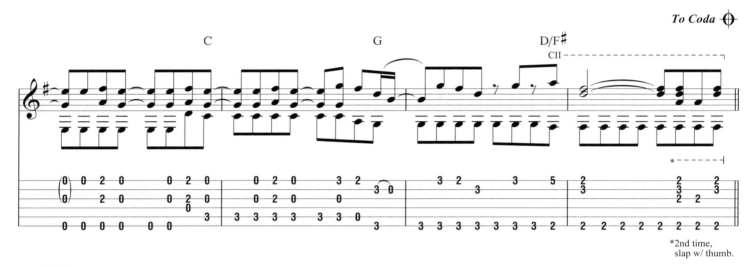

*2nd time,
slap w/ thumb.

C

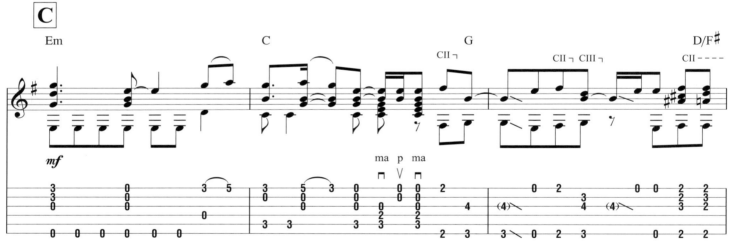

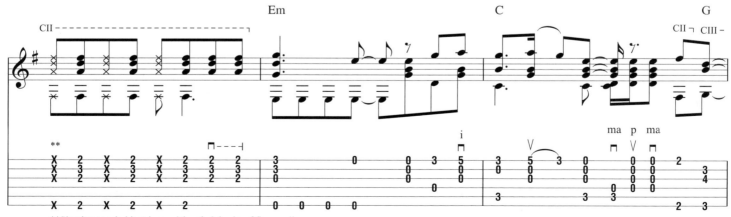

**Simultaneously hit strings w/ thumb & backs of fingernails
to produce a percussive sound, throughout.

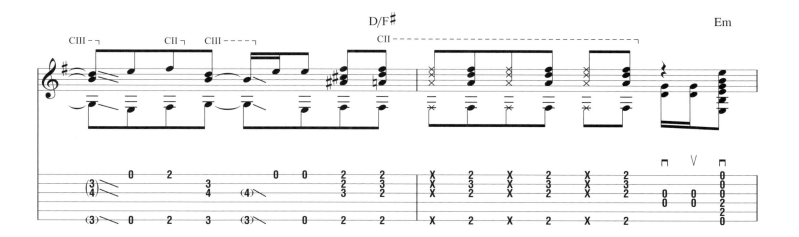

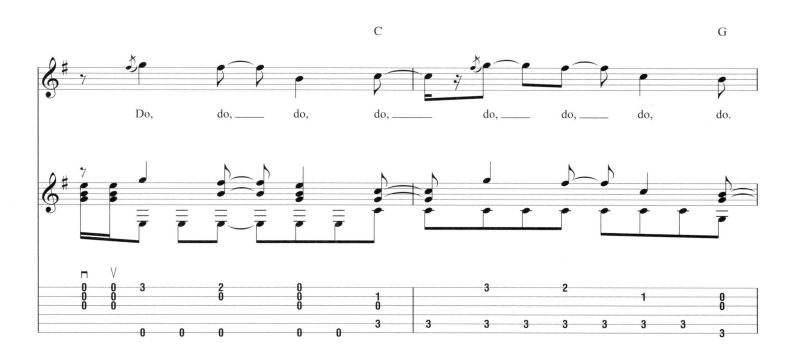

Coda

D

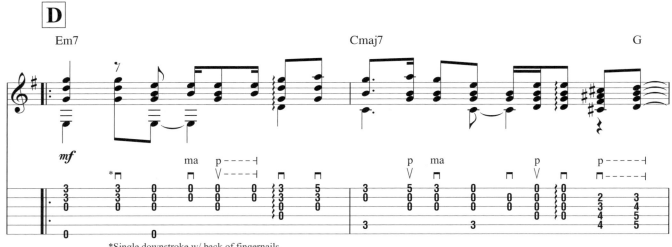

*Single downstroke w/ back of fingernails.

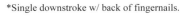

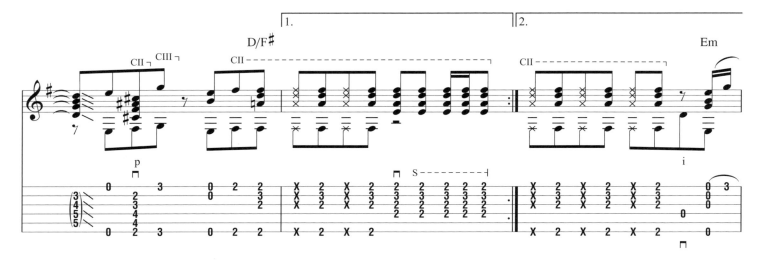

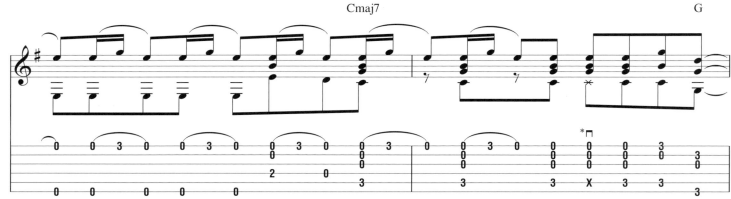

*In a single downstroke, sound upstemmed notes by striking strings w/ backs of fingernails while slapping thumb against strings to produce a percussive sound (downstemmed notes), throughout.

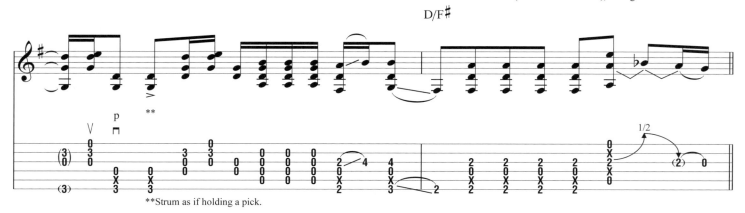

**Strum as if holding a pick.

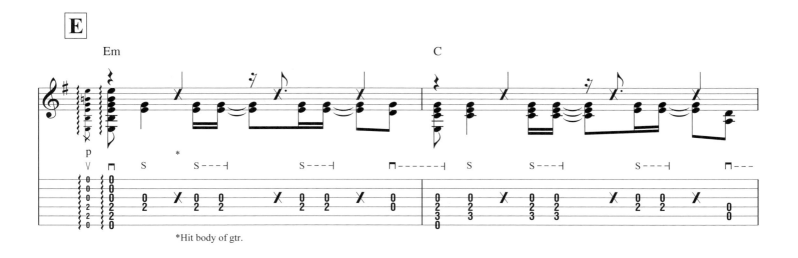

*Hit body of gtr.

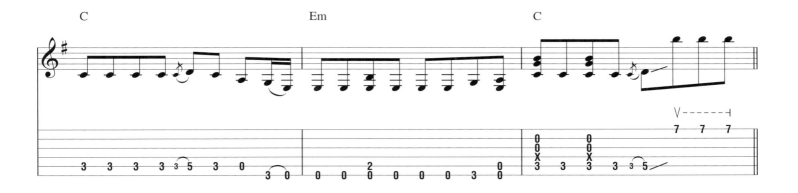

**Strum as if holding a pick, next 4 meas.

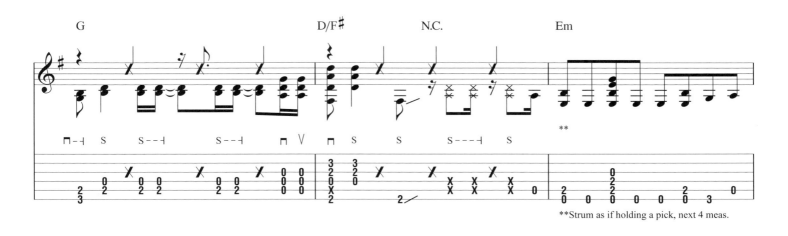

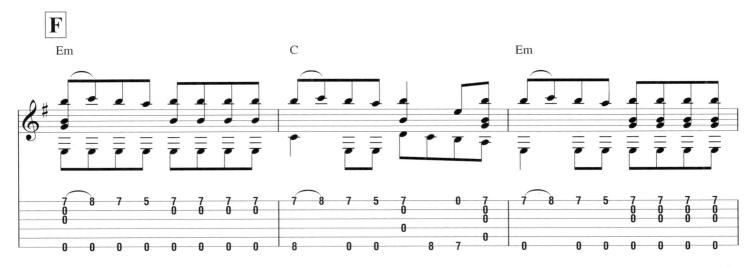

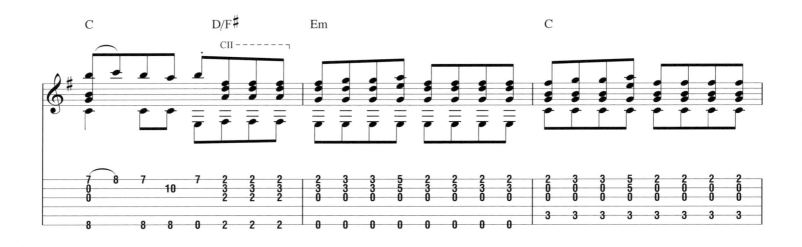

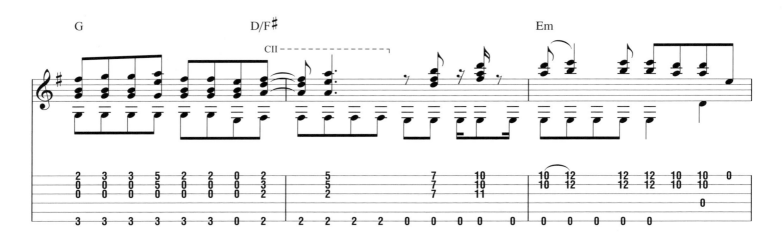

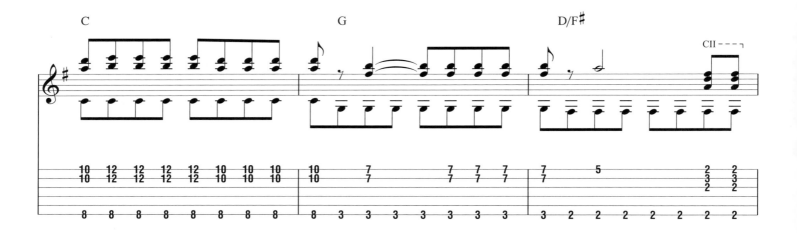

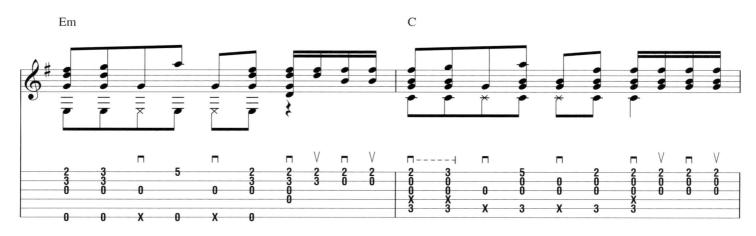

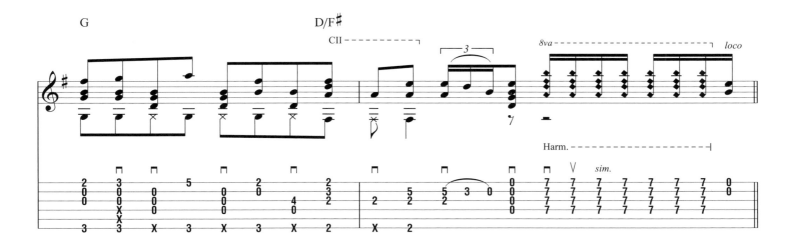

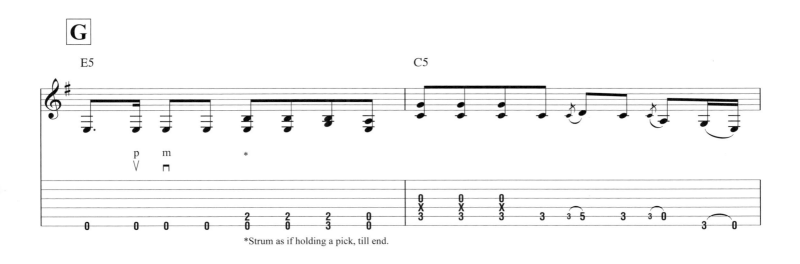

*Strum as if holding a pick, till end.

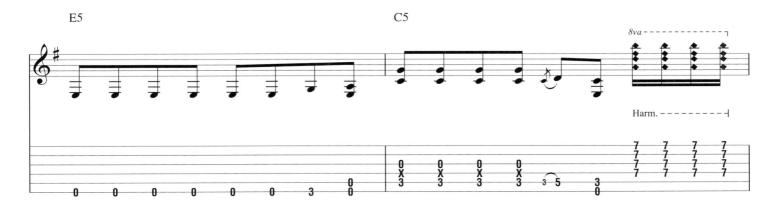

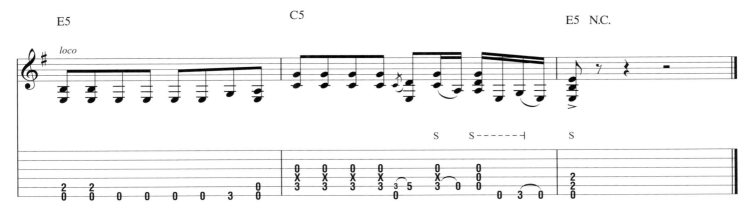

GUITAR NOTATION LEGEND

Guitar music can be notated three different ways: on a *musical staff*, in *tablature*, and in *rhythm slashes*.

RHYTHM SLASHES are written above the staff. Strum chords in the rhythm indicated. Use the chord diagrams found at the top of the first page of the transcription for the appropriate chord voicings. Round noteheads indicate single notes.

THE MUSICAL STAFF shows pitches and rhythms and is divided by bar lines into measures. Pitches are named after the first seven letters of the alphabet.

TABLATURE graphically represents the guitar fingerboard. Each horizontal line represents a string, and each number represents a fret.

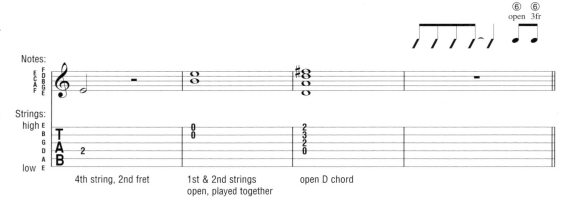

4th string, 2nd fret   1st & 2nd strings open, played together   open D chord

Definitions for Special Guitar Notation

HALF-STEP BEND: Strike the note and bend up 1/2 step.

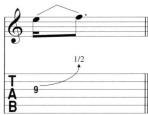

WHOLE-STEP BEND: Strike the note and bend up one step.

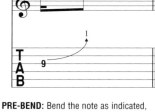

GRACE NOTE BEND: Strike the note and immediately bend up as indicated.

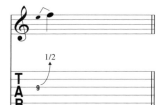

SLIGHT (MICROTONE) BEND: Strike the note and bend up 1/4 step.

BEND AND RELEASE: Strike the note and bend up as indicated, then release back to the original note. Only the first note is struck.

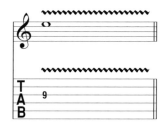

PRE-BEND: Bend the note as indicated, then strike it.

PRE-BEND AND RELEASE: Bend the note as indicated. Strike it and release the bend back to the original note.

UNISON BEND: Strike the two notes simultaneously and bend the lower note up to the pitch of the higher.

VIBRATO: The string is vibrated by rapidly bending and releasing the note with the fretting hand.

WIDE VIBRATO: The pitch is varied to a greater degree by vibrating with the fretting hand.

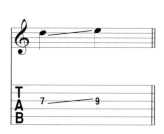

HAMMER-ON: Strike the first (lower) note with one finger, then sound the higher note (on the same string) with another finger by fretting it without picking.

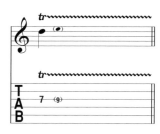

PULL-OFF: Place both fingers on the notes to be sounded. Strike the first note and without picking, pull the finger off to sound the second (lower) note.

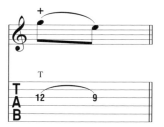

LEGATO SLIDE: Strike the first note and then slide the same fret-hand finger up or down to the second note. The second note is not struck.

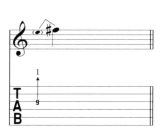

SHIFT SLIDE: Same as legato slide, except the second note is struck.

TRILL: Very rapidly alternate between the notes indicated by continuously hammering on and pulling off.

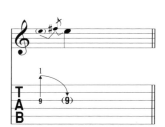

TAPPING: Hammer ("tap") the fret indicated with the pick-hand index or middle finger and pull off to the note fretted by the fret hand.

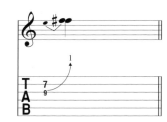

NATURAL HARMONIC: Strike the note while the fret-hand lightly touches the string directly over the fret indicated.

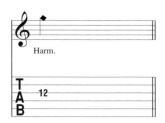

PINCH HARMONIC: The note is fretted normally and a harmonic is produced by adding the edge of the thumb or the tip of the index finger of the pick hand to the normal pick attack.

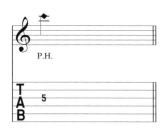

HARP HARMONIC: The note is fretted normally and a harmonic is produced by gently resting the pick hand's index finger directly above the indicated fret (in parentheses) while the pick hand's thumb or pick assists by plucking the appropriate string.

PICK SCRAPE: The edge of the pick is rubbed down (or up) the string, producing a scratchy sound.

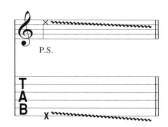

MUFFLED STRINGS: A percussive sound is produced by laying the fret hand across the string(s) without depressing, and striking them with the pick hand.

PALM MUTING: The note is partially muted by the pick hand lightly touching the string(s) just before the bridge.

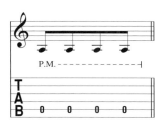

RAKE: Drag the pick across the strings indicated with a single motion.

TREMOLO PICKING: The note is picked as rapidly and continuously as possible.

ARPEGGIATE: Play the notes of the chord indicated by quickly rolling them from bottom to top.

VIBRATO BAR DIVE AND RETURN: The pitch of the note or chord is dropped a specified number of steps (in rhythm), then returned to the original pitch.

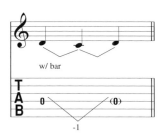

VIBRATO BAR SCOOP: Depress the bar just before striking the note, then quickly release the bar.

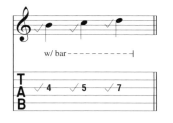

VIBRATO BAR DIP: Strike the note and then immediately drop a specified number of steps, then release back to the original pitch.

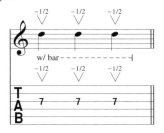

Additional Musical Definitions

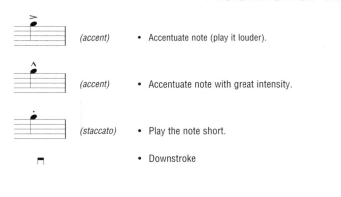

(accent)	• Accentuate note (play it louder).	
(accent)	• Accentuate note with great intensity.	
(staccato)	• Play the note short.	
⊓	• Downstroke	
V	• Upstroke	
D.S. al Coda	• Go back to the sign (%), then play until the measure marked "***To Coda***," then skip to the section labelled "**Coda**."	
D.C. al Fine	• Go back to the beginning of the song and play until the measure marked "***Fine***" (end).	

Rhy. Fig. • Label used to recall a recurring accompaniment pattern (usually chordal).

Riff • Label used to recall composed, melodic lines (usually single notes) which recur.

Fill • Label used to identify a brief melodic figure which is to be inserted into the arrangement.

Rhy. Fill • A chordal version of a Fill.

tacet • Instrument is silent (drops out).

• Repeat measures between signs.

• When a repeated section has different endings, play the first ending only the first time and the second ending only the second time.

NOTE: Tablature numbers in parentheses mean:
1. The note is being sustained over a system (note in standard notation is tied), or
2. The note is sustained, but a new articulation (such as a hammer-on, pull-off, slide or vibrato) begins, or
3. The note is a barely audible "ghost" note (note in standard notation is also in parentheses).

GUITAR *signature licks*

Signature Licks book/audio packs provide a step-by-step breakdown of "right from the record" riffs, licks, and solos so you can jam along with your favorite bands. They contain performance notes and an overview of each artist's or group's style, with note-for-note transcriptions in notes and tab. The CDs or online audio tracks feature full-band demos at both normal and slow speeds.

AC/DC
14041352.......................$22.99

AEROSMITH 1973-1979
00695106.......................$22.95

AEROSMITH 1979-1998
00695219.......................$22.95

DUANE ALLMAN
00696042.......................$22.99

BEST OF CHET ATKINS
00695752.......................$22.95

AVENGED SEVENFOLD
00696473.......................$22.99

BEST OF THE BEATLES FOR ACOUSTIC GUITAR
00695453.......................$22.99

THE BEATLES BASS
00695283.......................$22.95

THE BEATLES FAVORITES
00695096.......................$24.95

THE BEATLES HITS
00695049.......................$24.95

JEFF BECK
00696427.......................$22.99

BEST OF GEORGE BENSON
00695418.......................$22.95

BEST OF BLACK SABBATH
00695249.......................$22.95

BLUES BREAKERS WITH JOHN MAYALL & ERIC CLAPTON
00696374.......................$22.99

BLUES/ROCK GUITAR HEROES
00696381.......................$19.99

BON JOVI
00696380.......................$22.99

ROY BUCHANAN
00696654.......................$22.99

KENNY BURRELL
00695830.......................$22.99

BEST OF CHARLIE CHRISTIAN
00695584.......................$22.95

BEST OF ERIC CLAPTON
00695038.......................$24.99

ERIC CLAPTON – FROM THE ALBUM UNPLUGGED
00695250.......................$24.95

BEST OF CREAM
00695251.......................$22.95

CREEDANCE CLEARWATER REVIVAL
00695924.......................$22.95

DEEP PURPLE – GREATEST HITS
00695625.......................$22.99

THE BEST OF DEF LEPPARD
00696516.......................$22.95

DREAM THEATER
00111943.......................$24.99

TOMMY EMMANUEL
00696409.......................$22.99

ESSENTIAL JAZZ GUITAR
00695875.......................$19.99

FAMOUS ROCK GUITAR SOLOS
00695590.......................$19.95

FLEETWOOD MAC
00696416.......................$22.99

BEST OF FOO FIGHTERS
00695481.......................$24.95

ROBBEN FORD
00695903.......................$22.95

BEST OF GRANT GREEN
00695747.......................$22.99

THE GUITARS OF ELVIS – 2ND ED.
00174800.......................$22.99

BEST OF GUNS N' ROSES
00695183.......................$24.99

THE BEST OF BUDDY GUY
00695186.......................$22.99

JIM HALL
00695848.......................$22.99

JIMI HENDRIX
00696560.......................$24.99

JIMI HENDRIX – VOLUME 2
00695835.......................$24.95

JOHN LEE HOOKER
00695894.......................$19.99

BEST OF JAZZ GUITAR
00695586.......................$24.95

ERIC JOHNSON
00699317.......................$24.95

ROBERT JOHNSON
00695264.......................$22.95

BARNEY KESSEL
00696009.......................$22.99

THE ESSENTIAL ALBERT KING
00695713.......................$22.95

B.B. KING – BLUES LEGEND
00696039.......................$22.99

B.B. KING – THE DEFINITIVE COLLECTION
00695635.......................$22.95

B.B. KING – MASTER BLUESMAN
00699923.......................$24.99

MARK KNOPFLER
00695178.......................$22.95

LYNYRD SKYNYRD
00695872.......................$24.95

THE BEST OF YNGWIE MALMSTEEN
00695669.......................$22.95

BEST OF PAT MARTINO
00695632.......................$24.99

MEGADETH
00696421.......................$22.99

WES MONTGOMERY
00695387.......................$24.95

BEST OF NIRVANA
00695483.......................$24.95

VERY BEST OF OZZY OSBOURNE
00695431.......................$22.95

BRAD PAISLEY
00696379.......................$22.99

BEST OF JOE PASS
00695730.......................$22.95

JACO PASTORIUS
00695544.......................$24.95

TOM PETTY
00696021.......................$22.99

PINK FLOYD
00103659.......................$24.99

PINK FLOYD – EARLY CLASSICS
00695566.......................$22.95

BEST OF QUEEN
00695097.......................$24.95

RADIOHEAD
00109304.......................$24.99

BEST OF RAGE AGAINST THE MACHINE
00695480.......................$24.95

RED HOT CHILI PEPPERS
00695173.......................$22.95

RED HOT CHILI PEPPERS – GREATEST HITS
00695828.......................$24.99

BEST OF DJANGO REINHARDT
00695660.......................$24.95

BEST OF ROCK 'N' ROLL GUITAR
00695559.......................$19.95

BEST OF ROCKABILLY GUITAR
00695785.......................$19.95

BEST OF JOE SATRIANI
00695216.......................$22.95

SLASH
00696576.......................$22.99

THE BEST OF SOUL GUITAR
00695703.......................$19.95

BEST OF SOUTHERN ROCK
00695560.......................$19.95

STEELY DAN
00696015.......................$22.99

MIKE STERN
00695800.......................$24.99

BEST OF SURF GUITAR
00695822.......................$19.95

STEVE VAI
00673247.......................$22.95

STEVE VAI – ALIEN LOVE SECRETS: THE NAKED VAMPS
00695223.......................$22.95

STEVE VAI – FIRE GARDEN: THE NAKED VAMPS
00695166.......................$22.95

STEVE VAI – THE ULTRA ZONE: NAKED VAMPS
00695684.......................$22.95

VAN HALEN
00110227.......................$24.99

STEVIE RAY VAUGHAN – 2ND ED.
00699316.......................$24.95

THE GUITAR STYLE OF STEVIE RAY VAUGHAN
00695155.......................$24.95

BEST OF THE VENTURES
00695772.......................$19.95

THE WHO – 2ND ED.
00695561.......................$22.95

JOHNNY WINTER
00695951.......................$22.99

YES
00113120.......................$22.99

NEIL YOUNG – GREATEST HITS
00695988.......................$22.99

BEST OF ZZ TOP
00695738.......................$24.95

HAL•LEONARD®

www.halleonard.com

COMPLETE DESCRIPTIONS AND SONGLISTS ONLINE!
Prices, contents and availability subject to change without notice.

1016